KU-024-341

This is the exact opposite of what a book on acting should be, if indeed there should ever be such a thing. I suspect there should not.

Just for starters, acting means getting up off your behind and breathing life into the printed page. This book does just the reverse. Plucked out of the air, ripped from the mouths of gallant actors, squeezed back through the hoary old channels of analysis, and slapped back down onto a page, the words now lie gasping at the loss of their new-found freedom.

I have, therefore, to disabuse you. Although the genesis of this book lies in a so-called master class, acting is not, in fact, master class-able.

Music is. You need yourself and you need an instrument. The instrument you play is your means of communication; it serves as both your shield and your conduit. After a punishing training period lasting years and years and never quite finished, you are either able, technically speaking, to play the piece, or you are not. Whether you can then muster a magisterial interpretation is a matter of balancing the composer's intentions with your particular genius. You can learn by precept. Interpretation is a matter for negotiation and may be demonstrated to you without hurting your feelings too much, because your ego is marginally less at stake than your options.

Acting, however, like pain, is more a matter of opinion. You are your own instrument. There are really no technical absolutes for you to conquer. You require a text and yourself, but a self bared of defenses. When your acting is being dissected the criticism can appear to be aimed at you personally, when, in fact, it is directed at your interpretation. It is all too easy to lose sight of that distinction when your self-confidence wavers. No wonder, then, that the actor's ego can be a fragile thing, seeing itself as a mere matter for dispassionate discussion. Still, when all's said and done, it is your choice to put yourself on the line by being an actor, so you have no one but yourself to answer to for such unwelcome incursions into your privacy.

At worst, then, the process can be hurtful; at best, it can be pure joy, because that very personality of yours is illuminating a fictional one and making it sing. Music is not fictional; abstract, yes, but not fictional—it does not require an imaginative construct. Opera singers have the uplifting support of the music. Actors have only silence; no protection there.

Acting reaches into the inaccessible recesses of human behaviour, and requires you, while keeping your sanity, to be as mad as a hatter. There is no "open sesame" for these recesses; there are no special exercises analogous to playing scales; there are merely ways to approach it, aspects to be conscious of, techniques to absorb. The development of that awareness can take years of training, years of practise, but let's face it, the bottom line is that neither music nor acting can be taught unless you have an ear for it.

Some people want to be famous and earn pots of money. Others just want to live decently, with the more modest aim of becoming finer, simpler, better at what they do. Some people want to serve themselves; others want to serve the plays they inhabit. The two aims can, with luck and judgement, be combined, though that is rare.

Talking about acting is a contradiction in terms. It is a "doing" experience. (Like justice, it has to be *seen* to be done.) Hence my understandable caution about the value of such a book as this. Still, here we all are, and we shall examine how to approach a text, albeit in a very contracted form. There are ways to initiate the process, to open doors and look at what's behind them. Because we are looking at particularly wordy plays, those doors will be words: we can explore their meanings to give a character freshness, by means of *clarity of intention*. In Shakespeare, it is arguably true to say that text *is* character.

However, although we talk with words it is very difficult to talk, much less write, *about* words. And what lies between and beyond the words—the silences, and the meanings within meanings—are far too important to try to write down. Such things cannot be written. A major actor always has an innate apprehension of these layers of meaning, and although he cannot and probably should not articulate that knowledge, there's nothing to stop lively discussion of the means by which he apprehends: the text. The theoretical aspect of acting can be roughly communicated, but the experience of it cannot. I think it was Arthur Miller who advised: "Play the text, not what it reminds you of."

Shakespeare is words, words, words; a veritable monument to the great power of words. But he's not the Parthenon, you cannot walk around him to wonder at his indestructible symbolism, to gaze at his sublime proportions, to sigh over his half-spoiled splendours. No, the words have indeed lasted, as has the marble, but they are pliable and change their shape with each new tongue that speaks them. No good looking at them; you have to *do* them.

In the doing, the ultimate and only judgement is whether you believe what you see and hear. Is it "the truth"? I will not fall into the trap of trying to define what that might be. Edith Evans' anecdote will do for now: she once said that if a bolt of lightning were to strike her at any moment during a performance, she would hope that the resulting statue would appear just right for all eternity. Wishful thinking and hubris in about equal quantities there, I would say; but the nub of it is that she was constantly on a quest for theatrical truth. That truth, once achieved would, she hoped, be both arresting and unmistakeable.

I suppose you may hazard a guess that "the truth," whatever it is, becomes more possible the nearer the actor gets to his or her real, unprotected self. I shall leave it at that. Anyone who has been lucky enough to experience or witness it will know what I mean.

To my surprise, I once heard Frank Sinatra say in an interview that when he's working on a song the words come first; if he can make sense of the lyrics, he can sing the tune. I shouldn't have been surprised; his singing bears that out to perfection. Callas had the same sort of genius for letting us know the source of her pains and pleasures. With accuracy comes subtlety.

All performances are born in exploration, so we shall be looking at the parts to see how the whole might be got at. I shall be talking only of exploration in this class, not performance. Exploration is a matter of trying to do whatever it is that you're doing—better.

In the Beginning was the Word. The *idea* of the thing. Words, in an image-based age, can be all too easily devalued, yet language is, above all, the absolutely essential attribute of the human animal.

Images don't exactly help us to discern the richness of ambiguity. The glossy panoply of television, posters, computer screens pass endlessly before our eyes. We look, and move on thoughtlessly to the next picture, and the next. We are rarely haunted or troubled by the meaning of an image, except in very great films. Images come our way effortlessly. Words, however, need us to come to them. They need wooing, coaxing, cajoling, pondering. They lie there waiting for attention, like an anxious lover.

Rich, complex language is no longer the coin of the realm, so to speak; more reason still for us to "honour" that language. Cecily Berry, (who teaches voice and verse at the Royal Shakespeare Company) uses that word, and I can't think of a better way of putting it. Attention must be paid to it; not cursory attention, but prolonged and profound attention. If we don't, an unequaled dramatic literature will gradually become unapproachable and then unsayable. Eventually we will have it for academic reference only. What a lazy old loss that would be.

The pity of it is, the theatres where you can be apprenticed to your craft are obliged to present fewer and fewer classics due to a thoroughly un-visionary government arts policy. The depressing prevailing view that the arts are to be considered merely as cost-effective commodities has so depleted the theatrical landscape that young actors nowadays have little chance of honing their skills in anything but the most mundane fare. More depressing still, youngsters who want to train at accredited drama schools are all going to have to be the sons and daughters of rich Mrs. Worthington, since the grants have practically dried up. Middle-class gentility looms once again on the theatrical horizon. My old drama school, The London Academy of Music and Dramatic Art (LAMDA), reports that in 1992, 67 percent of students received discretionary awards, and in 1995, 70 percent of first-year students were fee-paying. That is a terrible rate of attrition. Worst of all, sight-reading tests are having to be introduced at auditions these days. What an indictment of a chronically messy educational system.

Short simple sentences, the sort you get on television or film, are really not that difficult to master. Acting as naturally as possible, propelled by these singularly unenlightening thoughts, is also not that difficult. But Shakespeare has more sustained ideas to communicate, and although the actor would wish to *appear* natural and unstrained, it is, in fact, not naturalistic acting at all that we are addressing here. It has another dimension altogether. Language of this order is as demandingly physical as a wordless Kung-Fu combat. It must be treated as being vibrantly alive, not dead, not symbolic—not the Parthenon.

Western classical theatre, unlike, say, the Japanese, is a word-based thing. So if you want to be that sort of an actor, then words are your passport. They tell us that things are not quite what they seem. That, in my view, is the stuff of drama: Things Are Not Quite What They Seem. Ambiguity; opposites jostling, in the same breath, for precedence. *Vorei e non vorei*—"I want to and I don't want to." If there is no internal struggle, there is no drama—merely fact. Theatre of this order, then, is metaphor.

Many years ago I watched a public master class given by Daniel Barenboim with a young Russian pianist. They were addressing a Beethoven piano sonata. First, the Russian played it for us in admittedly fine style: hair flying, nostrils flaring, shoulders digging into the notes like a bulldozer shifting rubble. Then, gently, Daniel began to point out to him that perhaps all this drama was rather obscuring the piece of music; too much "acting." We could clearly see the young pianist's intentions, and all very committed and passionate it was. But what, Daniel wondered, of Beethoven's intentions?

You may ask what *they* might be. Beethoven is dead; Shakespeare is dead. So how on earth can we possibly know what they meant? I mean, simply, that the performer mustn't stand too much in their way. A notice in the *London Times* of April 14, 1994, about the great pianist Alfred Brendel playing the complete cycle of Beethoven piano sonatas, will explain better: "...this audience is hearing increasingly more of Brendel than of Beethoven, and seems scarcely aware of it. Elements which once made Brendel's playing sharply characterised and distinctive are now becoming heavy fingerprints that threaten to mask the face of Beethoven himself...an interpretative impasse seems to have been reached, and the way forward is unclear." Even a very great artist can sometimes lose the way.

It is not up to the genius to explain himself; we as performers, however, must. The genius might not even suspect what endless richness lies in his work; it is up to us to discover it. To use a term of Ibsen's, we must "mine" the work. Interpretation has to be based on clear understanding, and the process of selection is what exploratory work is about. Why choose this reading over that? Why one emphasis over another? In a way it's like being a detective; the clues are all there on the page, as words or as notes. You have to follow the trail so that a cohesive view emerges, defensible in court.

Shakespeare, Beethoven, whoever, composed. We must "decompose." The English equivalent of Barenboim's German word may sound a little alarming, but the process isn't. It's fun.

When we read a newspaper, the political commentary becomes an interpretation of what lies behind a politician's latest speech. It is as if the speech is given in a code that then has to be unraveled and translated and its intention deciphered. Establishment double-speak and political correctness, are, of course, the prevailing obfuscations in public life. Nevertheless, you get my point; people hardly ever say what they mean. All of life, both public and private, becomes an unending quest to "read" people's true intentions. In this respect, at least, life and art are closer than we think.

Let us take the simple example of Celia to Rosalind in their first scene together in *As You Like It*.

I pray thee, Rosalind, sweet my coz, be merry.

Sounds harmless enough, but give it its due; there's something a little desperate here. How many clues? Three of them are easy; the sad girl is Celia's cousin and her name is Rosalind.

What more? Exasperation, pleading, or teasing in that "I pray thee"? Three very different moods. The formality of "I pray thee" also tells us this is a rather unusual mood for a familiar cousin to be in.

"Sweet my coz" tells us how Rosalind normally is. Or does it tell us Celia is cajoling, or even flattering, her cousin?

"Be merry" indicates some extremity; a word at the opposite end of the scale to "depressed." It implies, I would say, that Rosalind has been gloomy longer than is bearable to someone who is not gloomy.

Conclusion? It would appear to be both truthful and consistent if Celia were to be suppressing some impatience; amused, maybe, but somewhat fed up. A bantering familiarity of that sort would inform us of their closeness instantly, and the play will bear it out. Best of all, it spares us any girlish sweetness, and the play will bear that out, too. These are not just close friends, they are blood relations who have been brought up together, and they have A Problem. We shall soon learn what that problem is.

So there, in just nine words, we have Shakespeare, the master playwright, giving us of a host of informative facts with stunning economy. The nearest thing to it might be Jane Austen's opening to *Pride and Prejudice*: "It is a truth universally acknowledged that a single man in possession of a good fortune, must be in want of a wife." The story has begun . . .

Which brings us to the matter of comedy in Shakespeare. I don't think I'm up to defining it. Let's say, then, that for the purposes of acting there is no definable difference in the way you explore a comedy or a tragedy. In any case, in Shakespeare preeminently, light and shadow are so exquisitely intermingled that there are tears in *Twelfth Night*, laughter in *Lear*.

In the comedies, there lurks a melancholy which needs to be kept at bay by kicking against it. When Rosalind shrugs off Jaques' gloom with "I had rather have a fool to make me merry than experience to make me sad; and to travel for it too," she expresses the sentiments of all young lovers thirsty for life. It's not that the comedies are uproariously funny all the way through, but that youth struggling for experience makes us smile rather than frown.

The essential difference in the actor's attitude will derive from the understanding that, in a tragedy, death is inevitable; in a comedy, life is. The ordeal of gaining self-knowledge (the story of the play) is essentially the same ordeal in both forms. In the former, self-knowledge comes just too late to transform what life there is left by its revelation. In the latter, happily, it is never too late for changed perceptions to inform the future life of the protagonists.

The knowledge of death or of life will instinctively inform the way the actor proceeds on the stage during the course of the play. The regenerative twinkle of life and love gleams in the innocent eye of comedy; the mark of doom crouches fatefully on the questioning forehead of tragedy. The comic protagonist is always amongst friends; the tragic journey is a lonely one. Or let's say this: comedy has a healthy feeling to it, as if the protagonists had really big appetites. I like to think that if you served them a meal in the middle of the play, they'd drop everything to gulp it down. There's no such stomach for food in a tragedy; too much anguish in the belly, too many problems to grapple with.

These visceral adjustments in approach come as naturally to an actor as writing on a blackboard does to a teacher; the size of the handwriting is accommodated to the size of the space available. In a play, we are talking about interior space.

And these inner landscapes affect the light in the actor's eye, as it were. With fate growling at your heels you seem thus; with love tugging at your heartstrings, thus. A myriad subtleties lie in between. I seem to be describing a prevailing mood, and that will suffice. The tenor the actor works in will send the requisite message to the audience, and will help to determine the style of the piece. To be really simplistic: think of the ancient masks of comedy and tragedy, one with a smile, one with a frown. You may elect to treat comedy as if it were tragedy, or tragedy as if it were comedy, which is never a bad thing to do since both forms, in Shakespeare, require an equal emotional investment.

The notion of demonstrating how an actor should physically behave, given a certain historical period, is not particularly revealing. In a Restoration play, for example, you'd be an ass not to hold your arms so the lace cuff doesn't fall into the soup, or walk with the feet turned a little outward for balance on those red-heeled shoes. You'd be hard-put to manage a slouch in a corset and stomacher; or, conversely, not to feel rather at home in boys' clothes in a *travesti* part. There is no such thing as absolute authenticity on the stage; it is merely a matter of our adjusted aesthetic sense. The important thing is to feel comfortable rather than self-conscious.

Talking of which, many years ago (before any of you were born, I daresay) I was doing *Love's Labour's Lost* at Stratford-on-Avon, directed by John Barton. He was in a "let's do this authentically" phase, and decided we must all look thoroughly Elizabethan. Well, came the day of the first dress-rehearsal, and we found ourselves shoe-horned into appallingly uncomfortable corsets and stomachers, with shaven foreheads and no eyebrows; dead spits of the Virgin Queen without the perks. The boys looked great; glossy curls, peacock clothes, "sighing like furnace" to their mistress' eyebrow, for all the world like Nicholas Hilliard miniatures. Glenda Jackson, who was playing the Princess of France, and I, who was playing Rosaline (neither of us known to be shrinking violets), went on strike. "We can't breathe," we wheezed, "we can't move." "Nonsense," said John. "We look ugly," we whined. "Nonsense," said John. (We did, though.) At that moment, one of the girls gave a little sigh, and fell to the ground in a faint. Proof positive! Instead of ministering to her, we pointed dramatically at the heap of brocade on the floor and cried "You see! You see! We'll all die of suffocation!" John was forced to relent. We returned from our dressing rooms with loosened corsets and somewhat restored features, and the play proceeded as we'd rehearsed it, instead of

Photo by T. F. Holte, A.I.B.P. A.R.P.S.

Love's Labour's Lost: Glenda Jackson as the Princess and
Janet Suzman as Rosaline (Stratford, 1966)

being inhabited by wax-work replicas of the first Elizabeth. So
much for authenticity on the stage.

I digress; we must return to our sheep. It will be the words
that will provide the information you need. The nearer you get
to feeling that the words are yours, the more naturally your
body will respond. Hands that feel like bits of flailing meat will
stop trying to describe what your mind can't yet fully express

Hamlet
Act III, Scene ii

HAMLET: Speak the speech, I pray you, as I pronounced it to you, trippingly on the tongue: but if you mouth it, as many of your players do, I had as lief the town-crier spoke my lines. Nor do not saw the air too much with your hand, thus; but use all gently: for in the very torrent, tempest, and, as I may say, whirlwind of passion, you must acquire and beget a temperance that may give it smoothness. O, it offends me to the soul to hear a robustious periwig-pated fellow tear a passion to tatters, to very rags, to split the ears of the groundlings, who, for the most part, are capable of nothing but inexplicable dumb shows and noise: I would have such a fellow whipped for o'erdoing Termagent; it out-herods Herod: pray you avoid it.

PLAYER: I warrant your honour. [*A very patient actor here, humouring the Prince.*]

HAMLET: Be not too tame neither, but let your own discretion be your tutor: suit the action to the word, the word to the action; with this special observance, that you o'erstep not the modesty of nature: for anything so overdone is from the purpose of playing, whose end, both at the first and now, was and is, to hold, as 'twere, the mirror up to nature; to show virtue her own feature, scorn her own image, and the very age and

(*Scene continues on p. 16*)

and return to your control. Hamlet's advice to the players (which they probably didn't need) is still worth considering as a piece of profound common-sense. [See facing page.] The most salient of his points is to suit the action to the word, the word to the action. Easier said than done, I confess.

The British are a word-mongering nation, and they have been busy writing plays for half a thousand years. Long before movies did it on celluloid, they painted pictures with words. The Renaissance in Italy exploded with paintings and sculptures, buildings and murals; the Renaissance in England exploded with words. Their first theatres were small, not Epidauros-sized, so their tongues did more work than their gestures. Elizabethan plays are more about extravagantly human human beings than about gods and heroes.

In the late twentieth century the wheel has come full circle; the close-up in film has given us a taste for seeing the whites of the eyes. Acting is less grandiose and gestural than it once used to be; huge Victorian theatres are potential money-spinners rather than hosts to happy actors having a great time with great plays. But a division is widening; small theatres seem to denote "serious" plays; large ones fun, spectacle, "entertainment," as if "serious" plays cannot be "entertaining" and vice versa. Phooey! Only the two large auditoria of The Royal Shakespeare Theatre and The Royal National Theatre, where "serious" plays can be dished up in an "entertaining" way, save us from perdition.

So there is a downside to the influence that film has exerted on the tastes of mass audiences. (Aficionados will still go to

(Scene continued from p. 14)

body of the time his form and pressure. Now, this overdone or come tardy off, though it make the unskilful laugh, cannot but make the judicious grieve; the censure of the which one must, in your allowance, o'erweigh a whole theatre of others. O, there be players that I have seen play,—and heard others praise, and that highly,—not to speak it profanely, that, neither having the accent of Christians, nor the gait of Christian, pagan, nor man, have so strutted and bellowed that I have thought some of nature's journeymen had made men, and not made them well, they imitated humanity so abominably.

PLAYER: I hope we have reformed that indifferently with us, sir. [*Teaching your grandmother to suck eggs, sir.*]

HAMLET: O, reform it altogether. And let those that play your clowns speak no more than is set down for them: for there be some of them that will themselves laugh, to set on some quantity of barren spectators to laugh too; though, in the meantime, some necessary question of the play be then considered: that's villainous, and shows a most pitiful ambition in the fool that uses it. Go, make you ready.

the "great reckonings in little rooms.") And that is the desire for visual thrills in the theatre, which means that the designer often now takes pride of place as the informing influence on the presentation of a play. You may ask why that should be considered a minus rather than a plus; what's so bad about hydraulics, spectacular stage effects, revolves, and all the mechanics that Inigo Jones would have killed for? In itself, nothing; it is an excellent thing that design has become so adventurous and technically expert, but there are no gains without losses. What it means is that an audience expects to be entertained visually, and their ears and minds take a rest. Their attention to ideas, to debate, to moral tussles, to the panoply of the human condition has diminished in direct proportion to the glamour of the scenery. They have become less tuned-in to subtlety and to the excellence of language as a purveyor of excitement. Plays that were once troubling and emotional experiences have become not thought-provoking but eye-provoking artifacts. Musicals with sets so expensive that they could underwrite the rebuilding of Soweto rule the roost. More modest plays have to try to keep their end up in this visually competitive world, and the actor himself is no longer the *raison d'etre* of a drama; he is more a creature to be moved about on the set. All this means that the repertory system, once the granary of the theatrical landscape, can no longer provide the fodder of experience in the classics to young actors that they once used to be able to. Regional theatres simply can't afford to keep a resident company and to train them with a diet of chewy plays that will sharpen their acting teeth. Actors need a period of apprenticeship just as badly as young doctors, cabinet-makers, stone-masons, and indeed any profession that requires natural instinct to be tempered with solid experience.

Shakespeare has cast his gargantuan shadow across the aeons, not just because of *Hamlet* (that would suffice), but because he wrote another thirty-five spell-binders. That shadow is both a blessing and a curse: a blessing because it provides a touchstone for great dramatic writing; a curse because it seems impossible to do it better. The plays may be flawed and rambling, but they are superbly actable.

The upshot of this is that Shakespeare is regarded with far too much awe. His achievement and his reputation seem to frighten people off; all that old-fashioned language, all that dreaded blank verse. But if a play of his is excitingly and truthfully performed you won't have a better time in the theatre. They are at their very best as ensemble works, rather than star vehicles, so it is vital that each and every member of the cast feels at home with the language. The trouble comes when a play of his is indifferently done, and you've got three hours of declamation and mediocrity to squirm through. Peter Brook says it succinctly: "Deadly theatre bludgeons people into believing that boredom is honourable."

The fright probably starts at high-school or college. Instead of acting it you are required to read it, write about it, be examined on it. Worse, you have to be sitting to do these tasks. I would go so far as to say that Shakespeare, from a sitting position, is a bore; stand up and speak it and a host of complexities become clearer.

Complexity is part of the fun anyway; it's a coward who is put off by complexity. Certainly Shakespeare can bear any amount of intellectual examination, as miles and miles of library shelves will groaningly attest to; but add emotion and instinct to the cocktail and you're back to where the plays began their lives—not on dusty shelves, but in dusty theatres.

Let's look for a moment at an innocuous little line from *Antony and Cleopatra*. Octavius Caesar enters Cleopatra's monument and asks "Which is the Queen of Egypt?" It seems, at first glance, to be incredibly rude, as if he were trying to belittle her. Surely the Queen of Egypt would be easy to spot? What on earth game he is playing? Why would he so foolishly risk her anger, since he has actually come all the way from Rome to woo her? To insult her would be to defeat the reason for his mission.

All becomes clear in the playing: the poor fellow is ushered into this shadowy Egyptian monument to be greeted by three

Antony and Cleopatra: Janet Suzman as Cleopatra
and Rosemary McHale as Charmian (Stratford, 1973/4)

groveling figures all dressed pretty much alike. (It is only much later in the scene that Cleopatra says "Show me, my women, like a Queen.") How is Caesar to know her? He has never seen her before in the flesh, and reports of her "beggar all description." Now he is confronted by a group of bewilderingly beggarly females. Rather like the shock you get when there is one less step than you anticipated; Caesar had expected to see a mighty Queen, but instead he sees someone deliberately mocking her loss of position by mocking him.

A victorious Emperor is discomfited; a defeated Queen takes pleasure in a momentary revenge. The imperial embarrassment would be extreme. And so the line "Which is the Queen of Egypt," in context, is actually one of genuine confusion. The boot is on the other foot.

Treat Shakespeare as a playwright rather than an Author, and things fall more easily into place.

Actors need not be wary of analysis. It's vital for verse. It's also a lot of fun, and won't squash your instincts if it is used to further an understanding of what's going on. When you have explored all the possible alternatives, you can tuck them away and settle for the one that, in your view, best serves the character. That way you can justify your choice, if need be. If you don't know why you are doing something, stop and ask yourself. Maybe there isn't an answer. It doesn't matter. The curiosity was there, and curiosity is a lovely trait. It means the actor is alive to small nuances, shifts, clues. An incurious actor is a limited actor.

Our Russian pianist, having chosen to end an arpeggio on a thundering crescendo, was surprised when Barenboim suggested that Beethoven might, just might, have been intending a more delicate suspiration to lead into the quiet passage that followed...perhaps a sudden diminuendo in preference to a crescendo? The difference, when the young man tried this new dynamic, was exquisite because it was unexpected and delicate. It felt (dare I say it?) truthful. In other words, it was not an obvious alternative. Obviousness dulls the senses; logic sharpens them.

At first glance, Caesar's line seems insulting, but thought through logically, in context, it becomes the opposite. In that way the scene kicks off to a fresh and dramatic start.

The person who can write a play that still coruscates four hundred years after it was thought up deserves not a jot less than our most vigilant attention. What on earth makes us think we can interpret such works without trying every imaginable way to give them contemporary life? No cobwebbery, please, no received ideas, no clichés, no intonings, no false grandeur.

Each performer is special, certainly, but Shakespeare is more special. More is expected of you. The chief pleasure of classical acting is precisely this: to ask more of yourself than you thought was in you. If you want an easy life, stick to television.

I once heard an old recording of Henry Ainley doing the St. Crispin's Day speech from *Henry V*. Musically speaking, he went up a semi-tone on each line, deliberately raising the temperature, and culminating in the great rallying cry of "...upon St. Crispin's daaayyy!" (Laurence Olivier later took this idea and made it his own.) In our more technocratic (more heartless?) age, such verse-music is no longer "in." At Stratford in the early sixties, Peter Brook, Peter Hall, and John Barton—University men—encouraged in my generation of actors a less romantic

As You Like It

Act III, Scene iv

ROSALIND: Never talk to me; I will weep.

CELIA: Do, I prithee; but yet have the grace to consider that tears do not become a man.

ROSALIND: But have I not cause to weep?

CELIA: As good cause as one would desire; therefore weep.

ROSALIND: His very hair is of the dissembling colour.

CELIA: Something browner than Judas's: marry, his kisses are Judas's own children.

ROSALIND: I' faith, his hair is of a good colour.

CELIA: An excellent colour: your chestnut was ever the only colour.

ROSALIND: And his kissing is as full of sanctity as the touch of holy bread.

CELIA: He hath bought a pair of cast lips of Diana: a nun of winter's sisterhood kisses not more religiously; the very ice of chastity is in them.

ROSALIND: But why did he swear he would come this morning, and comes not?

CELIA: Nay, certainly, there is no truth in him.

ROSALIND: Do you think so?

(Scene continues on p. 24)

and more rational approach to verse-speaking: meaning takes precedence over beautiful sounds. The cobwebs were brushed away. Great actors brush them off instinctively anyway; a film clip I saw once of Eleanora Duse showed her to be a very modern actor indeed: economical, truthful, detailed.

Naturally gifted performers, in all disciplines, have an instinctive feel for timing and phrasing. For those less gifted, a firm knowledge of structure and an inquiring mind won't do any harm. In any case, it seems a sensible idea to decide what you are about before letting it rip. Form without content is arguably more irritating than the other way around.

There is a kind of élan, a generous tumult, to an actor who has good breath control and who is able, therefore, to follow an idea through to its end without breaking it up to regather his forces. That kind of sweep is important in Shakespeare: clarity, speed, and emotional commitment. But in order to do that *without generalising* you have to know what you're saying. Spade work; let's dig. Or, as musicians often say, "let's play the ink." I suggest we dip into Act III, Scene iv of *As You Like It* to see what the ink might tell us. [See facing page.]

ROSALIND: Never talk to me; I will weep.

CELIA: Do, I prithee; but yet have the grace to consider that tears do not become a man.

If Rosalind is on first, speaking as she comes, we may infer that she is stage-managing Poetic Silence while she Suffers . . .

OR that she is running from Celia to look for a private place where she can have a Good Cry in peace; Celia, following, has no intention of uttering a word; she's resigned to a Scene . . .

(Scene continued from p. 22)

CELIA: Yes; I think he is not a pickpurse nor a horse-stealer; but for his verity in love, I do think him as concave as a covered goblet or a worm-eaten nut.

ROSALIND: Not true in love?

CELIA: Yes, when he is in; but I think he is not in.

ROSALIND: You have heard him swear downright he was.

CELIA: Was is not is: besides the oath of a lover is no stronger than the word of a tapster; they are both the confirmers of false reckonings. He attends here in the forest on the duke, your father.

ROSALIND: I met the duke yesterday, and had much question with him. He asked me of what parentage I was; I told him, of as good as he; so he laughed and let me go. But what talk we of fathers when there is such a man as Orlando?

CELIA: O, that's a brave man! he writes brave verses, speaks brave words, swears brave oaths and breaks them bravely, quite traverse, athwart the heart of his lover; as a puisny tilter, that spurs his horse but on one side, breaks his staff like a noble goose: but all's brave that youth mounts and folly guides.—Who comes here?

OR Celia has every intention of speaking and Rosalind preempts her, sensing a lecture...

OR Celia is on first, looking for a quiet spot for a siesta, say, and tumultuous Rosalind can't bear to be ignored...

Whatever...

The extravagance of "Never" (rather than plain "do not") tells us these are rather more crocodilish than real tears.

"I will weep" implies self-justification ("I know I'm a pain in the ass but I can't help crying")...

OR sulkiness ("Leave me alone, I have to Suffer")...

OR operatic self-dramatisation ("Say nothing; observe my Suffering")...

OR a reply to a sensible admonition ("I am beyond reason")...

Whatever...

But what if the actress, shying from any comic extravagance, would prefer to play this line very quietly and grievously? Would it not transport us to another sort of play, one in which Rosalind was in real pain? I would suggest "no" to this choice, for two reasons: one, comedies need to get on with it, so eschew indulgences that don't advance the story; and two, how would you get out of that mood quickly enough for the scene to continue without trivialising the pain?

So, it would appear that deeply felt "real" emotion would send the wrong signals, which would justify our saying that there is a kind of extravagance here. In any case, Celia's reply, at once dry and sensible, would jolt us back into Arden by mocking a forgetful Rosalind into remembering the play-acting mode, their necessary camouflage in this unpredictable forest. Paradoxically, "play-acting" implies a certain amateurish dramatic extravagance.

These two speeches also show us how very different the two girls are; the one passionate and talkative, the other teasing and watchful.

The comedies invariably involve people falling in love, often quite suddenly, and always to the hilt. Love sends adrenaline coursing through the system. Adrenaline means your mind works like lightning. The mind working fast and furiously means there is no time for pausing until it is absolutely necessary. Emotions are raw, leaping to wrong conclusions highly probable. (Look how avidly Claudio swallows the absurd bait offered him in *Much Ado*, chauvinist piglet that he is.)

It's as if people are kissed awake by love, just as the fairy tales say. Celia is largely unexcitable because she's got nothing to be excited about; her turn will come. I suspect Celia is quite sleepy a lot of the time; she says it not once but twice in the play. I shouldn't like to be too whimsical, but love generates tremendous energy, and the lack of it induces the opposite, a certain lethargy of the spirit. So, until Celia's questionable prince comes along and "kisses" her awake, she's busy making herself comfortable on some tussock or other.

This difference—in nature, in energy, in emotional investment—between the smitten and the un-smitten should naturally dictate the tenor of their scenes together. That is why if you find yourself catching someone else's tone in a play it is invariably an indication that character is slipping.

Playing together is Newtonian: every action should elicit an equal and opposite reaction. There is no better relationship in all the comedies for that wayward duality than that between Celia and Rosalind.

Moreover, if I'm right about the protagonists in a comedy possessing a life-enhancing assurance about their own immortality, then Celia's put-downs will never be mean-spirited or ungenerous, merely mischievous. Playfulness is always the most watchable thing; there is always another agenda going on behind playfulness, and that is an immensely intriguing quality in the theatre. You can be playful in tragedy, too.

Shakespeare loves a bit of mischief. Like a champion tennis player, he enjoys trying to wrong-foot his characters to see how they will recover their balances. See what fun he has confusing Octavius Caesar, or Viola when she visits Olivia.

Perhaps the quality that most informs Shakespeare's comedic creations is a certain humorous humanity; naughtiness, if you like. The Rosalind that can say "Sell when you can, you are not for all markets"—and that in the full spate of her anger at Phoebe's pitiless frankness—is the one to find.

But I digress; back to the ink.

"Do, I prithee; but yet have the grace to consider that tears do not become a man" is Celia's reply to Rosalind's self-indulgence.

"Grace" is usually applied to girls; "consider" is something you can only do when you are calm; "become" has a double edge, since Rosalind has "become" a man by dressing as one, but her girlish tears do not suit the disguise. So Celia transforms her from girl to boy in one swingeing sentence.

Is this not the subtlest way of saying "pull yourself together"? Is it not the most courteous display of feminine psychology: formality with affection, firmness with humour?

But what about another reading of the line? Could Celia possibly be bored with Rosalind's histrionics? That, I fear would ill-serve the play. Boredom is a most delicate matter. Characters must beware of acting "being bored." (See Stanislavski.)

Playing "being bored" is boring to play on a sustained level. Boredom is something that happens to you, not something you can make happen. It is passive rather than active. Besides, it would tempt the audience into imagining the bored as boring; an unfair indictment to inflict on a hard-working protagonist.

Let's see how we could transform "boredom" into something contributory rather than destructive:

If Celia's desire to snooze overcame her desire to observe her cousin at play, her "boredom" would then become amusing rather than judgemental. Her character's needs would thereby become as real as Rosalind's needs, albeit more mundane. She'd have to fight against her sleepiness, and that might become an entertaining little struggle to witness. Still, she is there in each love scene to be a witness as well as a chaperone, and were she to nod off I guess Rosalind would wake her up, rather cross that her performance as Ganymede was being missed. Certainly Celia would be up to *pretending* to nod off as a comment on her cousin's excesses, which would inject a nice note of astringency into the proceedings.

What I am saying is that acting "bored" must be a positive rather than a negative action. Chekhov's people are particularly famous for telling us how bored they are, how tired they are. Even so, do we take that at face value? Stanislavski's Damascene revelation was that the characters don't *know* they are bored. Therefore their self-confessed inertia must be transmuted by the actor into frustration or irritation or tears—something temperamental rather than passively moody. Just so with playing drunk: play trying to be sober. Same with dying: try not to. (It's what real people do.) Think opposites. Think how people laugh when they cry and cry when they laugh. Acting is active.

All too often, there can be a quality of archness, or knowingness, that creeps into the playing of comedy. Unless the character is, in essence, a nauseatingly arch sort, it is advisable to avoid this. Shakespearean comedy thrives best on openness and unself-consciousness.

Rosalind says of Orlando's hair:

I' faith, his hair is of a good colour.

Celia's reply is:

An excellent colour: your chestnut was ever the only colour.

If Celia makes like she really and truly believes in the lip-smacking beauty of chestnut, it will probably be funny. If she sounds like she's leading Rosalind on, it will probably not; it will sound arch.

It is the oddest thing; when you switch on the television or the radio, you know instantly if real people are being interviewed or if they are actors pretending to be real people. Why? For one thing, the actors sound almost too good to be true: too inflected, too colourful, too dramatic, too cogent. Real people speak more simply, even monotonously. Because they have genuinely experienced what they are talking about, reliving that experience, especially if it has been painful, may not be something they particularly want to do. They search for the words to describe it; there are fumblings and pauses. They can see, in their mind's eye, what they are describing, and want only to report the experience and get it out of the way quickly. There is a kind of numbness; the incident often sounds more dull than it actually was.

This being the fiftieth anniversary year of the liberation of the death camps, it is inevitable that one should have watched film after film of people recounting the worst tales ever told on the face of this earth. In Claud Landesmann's monumental work of investigation, *Shoa*, every single survivor of those evil places, every single person who witnessed the diabolical events, spoke quietly. Every now and then they would look away, as if shying away from the ghastly pictures seared onto their retinas. They would stop, in strong efforts to control the surges of feeling that choked them. On their faces were almost bemused half-smiles, as if they still couldn't believe the enormity of what they were recounting. Their voices were factual, low, deliberate. Their choice of words was simple, since there *are* no words to describe such things. They kept their privacy intact; anything more would have been an unbearable intrusion into that personal hell. Ordinary people must hug their sanity to themselves with ordinary words; life is much, much worse than art.

When Shakespeare depicts what it might be like to die (I'm thinking of Claudio in *Measure for Measure*) he does, for us all, what these people are unable to. That is what a poet must do—describe the indescribable.

The actor can but imagine the experience and his desire, by contrast, is to impart its inherent drama by heightening its impact. Hence the over-inflected speech. Sometimes one has to lower the impact.

Some actors have an aptitude for making quick sense of texts, and they rather enjoy colouring them with "meaningful" inflexions. But the real fascination is to find the motive for the choice of words; to search for the experience that gives rise to the choice of *that* particular word, and no other, to describe *that* experience, and no other.

The difference between indifferent and good acting is the desire in the actor for particularity.

Formal dramatic writing produces the same pitfalls. A text superficially absorbed produces generalised cadences and a surfeit of "acting." There is a surface pattern to a string of words which *appears* comprehensible when you hear it, if it is spoken with a good dose of flair and vocal dexterity, but the truth is that you don't really understand a word of it. You have the impression that you do, but actually you don't; you merely follow the *sound* of the words without comprehending their *source*. (This is fine for news-readers, who have no subtext to deal with, but it is not fine for the complexities of dramatic characters who may say one thing and mean another.) I'm always surprised, and a little saddened, at how easily some people can be taken in by a show-off performance. They simply don't know when they are being bamboozled. More fool they; the difference, in both a spectator and an artist, between a mind that is really engaged and one that is not, is immense.

In Shakespeare, the *choice* of words is always so special that, if you are even half awake, much of the work will have been done for you. Because of that, there is no need to "comment" on a word. Inexperienced actors often feel they must embellish with their bodies what they are saying with their mouths. They are not really listening to the text; cock your ear to the page, as it were, and you will "hear" what is being said. I repeat the musical injunction: play the ink.

For example, when Celia teases Rosalind with:

O that's a brave man! he writes brave verses, speaks brave words, swears brave oaths and breaks them bravely,...

there is no need to swagger, verbally or physically, on the word "brave." You'd be surprised how many people feel they have to. Trust. Trust the verse, trust the prose; it won't let you down.

If you get into a "tune" (the *sound* of a feeling rather than the feeling itself) and can't break it, stop yourself. Paraphrase, shake your shoulders, jump up and down, stand on your head, whisper the passage. (Whispering is always a good wheeze: it cuts out the voice and allows the unadorned meaning of the words to come out on the breath). Do, in fact, *anything* that will relax your body and reconcentrate your mind on exactly what is being said.

Actors need a sort of internal Geiger counter as they work, which bleeps every time they hit the bull's-eye and blows a raspberry every time they miss it. It takes courage to stop and question. But without courage, why act?

Actors are rather compliant people by nature, and often they too-readily wait for the director to comment. They don't want to spoil the flow. Well, OK, but judge for yourself, too. When you are "mining" a play, lift every stone to look for the worms squirming beneath, or for the gleam of the seam of gold. Directors are not infallible, and some are plain lazy; you could wait all day for a comment on something that is troubling you. I recently did a play with a director who couldn't be bothered with tiny moments of conflict between the characters that should have been explored but weren't. These unresolved, though adequately papered-over, cracks in the edifice were a continual irritant during the run of the play. It is a great help, however, if you have like-minded colleagues in the cast; a desire for clarity becomes suspiciously like making a fuss if you're on your own, and can be distinctly uncomfortable. This sort of thing shouldn't happen, and it is unpleasant to work divisively, but it's as well to know that, though rare, it does occur. Remember, the director doesn't have to live with the play; the actor does.

There is an unmistakeable feeling of pleasure when something works, and an equally unmistakeable feeling of being slightly ill-at-ease when something doesn't. These feelings should be listened to. Instinct is a great matter.

Sometimes a tiny change of emphasis will help a thought sit right.

When Rosalind says to Phebe, "Sell when you can, you are not for all markets," a stress on the word "all" would appear to be the obvious one. But it might help the wickedness factor if the "not" is touched in instead. I shouldn't like to be categorical about this, because each person will have their own way of working. If the line is confided to Phebe as an irritatingly fraternal piece of advice, "tough but honest," as it were, it will no doubt play itself.

It is all very well doing something right once (the joy of film), but in the theatre, getting it right again and again is the thing. The chances are obviously greatly increased if you know what on earth you're doing.

When civilians, if I may call them that, ask an actor how on earth he learns all those lines (an irritating question if ever there was one because it implies that that is the major difficulty in acting) the answer is simple: you remember them because you know exactly why you are saying them. You can mark out the shape and texture of a role at the first reading well enough, and first readings often have a kind of instinctive rightness to them. Do not be deceived, however: you won't be able to repeat that first fine careless rapture without a lot of hard work to help you capture and, most importantly, hold on to, that first instinctive response. Don't struggle to remember what it was that once happened to you when you are despairing of ever finding it again; it will come back in some form or other if you concentrate on what is happening *now*, right this second. Acting is only alive when it is concentrated *in the moment*.

The prolonged rigours of the stage are very different from the brief incandescence of film acting; repeating a performance nightly takes a terrible discipline, hence the groundwork I'm talking of. A face that is really concentrated is a beautiful thing to see. I think that is why athletes are so good to watch. And babies. They are in the moment.

I once shared a scene with an actress who had to come on and deliver a long speech about the horrid things that had happened to her during the day. It was written as a comical, end-of-tetherish speech; a frazzled speech which prepared the way for A Confession. (The name of the actress is immaterial, because it is the theory rather than the practise which I wish to discuss here.)

One night, towards the last few weeks of a six month run, something horrid must really have happened to her during the day, and she came on and delivered that same speech truly angry and truly frazzled. It took off and was fast and funny and full of feeling. Laughs came effortlessly where none had come before. "Oh, good," thought I, "she's finally cracked it." Not so, for the next night we had reverted back to the well-worn delivery. She had effectively forgotten what emotion had powered the speech the night before. In subsequent performances bits of the new attitude crept back shyly, like a half-remembered conversation, and once or twice she started off the scene with the spark that ignites, but it petered out before it should have. (As I have said elsewhere, *sustaining* an emotion for as long as it takes is the *sine qua non* of stage acting.)

Now, this is an interesting problem: why should a punctilious, experienced actress have such a fuzzy acting memory? Why was she not able to work out for herself what the difference was between mark 1 and mark 2? She was sure to know she could not reproduce the actual circumstances which had triggered her anger in the first place, but should have been able to re-create the semblance of the emotion at will. That is what an actor is required to do, after all.

The blame lies, in the first instance, with a lackadaisical rehearsal period. The motivation for the scene had not been settled on. We had never debated what the scene was *about*. The actress had been allowed her head, and very charming it was too. Actors often rely on their charm, and a heady addiction it can be. (In public life it has provoked the latter-day epithet we are all tiresomely tarred with, "luvviedom"—God help us!) More to the point, our actress had not been urged by the director to look for alternatives, and so she stuck with what came easiest; a certain measured, put-upon tone that was certainly amusing but not downright funny. On the night in question, her anger made her more vulnerable; that made her predicament more sympathetic to the audience; that set them free to laugh in recognition of an irritating day. Best of all, it was fast.

At the risk of repeating myself, when the blood is up the adrenaline flows, the mind is zinging, and the tongue rattles along. Bingo—you have *pace*. Speed probably comes to the same thing, but is an external command rather than an inner imperative, although actors always look immensely relieved when you just say to them "do it faster," rather than embarking on a tedious discourse on the character's blood pressure.

Now, it was not necessary for her to analyse all of the above, but it was necessary for her to realise that by being angry she had released the heart of the speech. More to the point, the ease with which she stormed through it must have given her a good feeling. The irritations of life had been transmuted into the pleasures of art (small "a"). She should have noted that, and in some quiet moments when she got home she should have been able to reason out what exactly had happened to transform the speech. But she was able to work out only part of the reason for the transformed delivery of this speech, judging by the intermittent way it came and went in subsequent performances.

It is very difficult to be objective about yourself as an actor. The director is there to enable the actor to settle on a simplified and defining over-view. He is watching it, you are doing it; big difference. There are times when I have been forced to rehearse while performing because rehearsals had been messy, and it is most unsatisfactory because you don't have the creative input of the other actors, and cannot work things out to suit their characters equally. And if you spring new things on some actors, they can't adjust themselves to it. Others can, and delight in having new things thrown at them. I personally rather like it, but many actors don't.

Much of what happens in a rehearsal room, and in performance, is thought about quietly in your head so that you go armed, the next day, with ideas you are eager to put into practise. In the car, in the bath, in bed, while cooking—anywhere where your imagination is free to concentrate will do. It can mean you burn the soufflé, get honked at on the green light, and commit other small catastrophes, but so what?

You see, the point is that once you have hit the bull's-eye, and the intention is rock-solid, there is nothing you cannot do within the parameters of your choice. If the parameters are fudged, you stick for dear life to what makes you feel safe; if they are solid, you can stick your neck out and be daring. Exciting acting is about being daring. I don't mean loud, or meretricious, I mean you push the parameters to their limits without endangering the intentions of the play as accepted by the director and his cast.

The reason I am urging you to stop yourselves, and ask yourself questions, and try different things in different ways, is because patterns of behaviour are very easy to adopt if they seem to come easily on your first go. There are, roughly speaking, three stages in working on texts:

l) the first fine careless flush,

2) the rejection of that as you get deeper in, and

3) the entrenchment of a *point of view*, which will allow you a second go, carefully constructed this time around, and therefore the freedom to be relaxed enough to do what you want.

If you are not given the opportunity to try out all sorts of alternate readings in rehearsal, how the hell do you know what's right? I am reminded of a famous Guinness advertisement which went like this: "I've never tried it 'cos I don't like it."

You will find that during the run of a play a myriad of discoveries, never mind how minuscule, are made by an actor every night. The greater the play, the more exciting those sudden apprehensions of a detail you had never noticed before. The drearier the play, the more you will seek them out, if only to keep yourself from going wild with boredom.

I asked Murray Perahia (one of the greatest of pianists) how he would feel if he were asked to play a Mozart piano concerto, say, eight times a week for six months. He blenched visibly. It is a most unreasonably exacting demand put upon actors, and for that reason you cannot hope to give the same intensity of performance eight times a week. One often feels guilty when a performance is below par on a given night, but there is damn-all you can do about it. I think Murray might have fainted clean away at the prospect of playing, say, Scott Joplin for such an unconscionable run.

Let us, for a moment, talk about the degrees of intensity of an emotion as applied to a comedy or a tragedy. The anger I was describing above could not be, in the context of this particular play, a searing, white-hot, ominously quiet thing. Nor could it be a glowing rage, sending out sparks, and shrivcling the leaves from the trees sort of thing. Had she been playing Lady Percy, or Cleopatra, that would have been fine. No, her instinct tempered that anger to comic proportions, so that it did not overwhelm the frailer bark. There was nothing wrong with her comic instinct, but her objective emotional memory was muddled.

I think that is the point; laughter instantly puts things into perspective. Comedy honours a sense of proportion; tragedy a sense of disproportion. Nothing is remediable in tragedy; the events unroll in an ineluctable way, and when this stygian vehicle rolls its terrible wheels over the helpless bodies of protagonists they know they cannot command its course. When Desdemona says "Do not talk to me, Emilia; / 1 cannot weep; nor answer have I none / But what should go by water," she knows she's done for. When Hamlet says "The time is out of joint—Oh cursed spite, / That ever I was born to set it right!" he knows he can't. When Macbeth says "Tomorrow, and tomorrow, and tomorrow," he knows there will be no tomorrows. They will struggle like hell to the very end not to be dead, like brave bulls, but go they must.

In Shakespeare, the line between the two can be disturbingly close; *Measure for Measure* without the Duke to re-jig things could be a tragedy. Polonius' muddled laundry-list tickled Shakespeare no end, I should imagine, since his plays are a wondrous mixture of "tragical-comical-historical-pastoral, scene undividable, or poem unlimited." It is a wild goose chase to try to find where Shakespeare himself stands on any issue, or where his sympathies lie with any character. He allows them their space, with all the sublime objectivity of a loving creator, but I can't help feeling that, in this instance at least, he is sending a message via Polonius about his delight in defying definition.

Nevertheless, and unsurprisingly, I believe that the divine Shakespeare can be judiciously cut and trimmed here and there without too much guilt. When an Elizabethan image is having a laboured gallop over the centuries, I think it is legitimate to give modern audiences a leg up. For example, the "brave" speech quoted earlier [p. 32] continues:

> ... quite traverse, athwart the heart of his lover; as
> a puisny tilter, that spurs his horse but on one
> side, breaks his staff like a noble goose: ...

Chivalric combat is surely too arcane an image to sustain before the delights of "noble goose" eventually arrives. Cut it; you'll be forgiven.

I directed a production of *Othello* in Johannesburg some years ago, and in order to spare the audience too many archaisms (Euro-centric claptrap might be the radical political view of such fusty stuff), I had little hesitation in cutting a few vexed passages or incomprehensible lines (which are usually the same thing). I even went so far as to change the odd word for a more accessible equivalent, as long as it scanned. Although the purists will doubtless shudder, a sense of contemporary freshness is like gold to an audience that doesn't give a damn about the sanctity of untouched texts.

If you truly heed (like our musicians—*listen* to the text) the prose-to-verse-and-back-to-prose surges in the plays, much of the work is done for you. For a start, prose and verse are printed differently on the page. As a general rule of thumb, prose is an outpouring, verse is a distillation. Prose is the "you" feeling, verse the "thou." Prose can be poetic, but verse is never prosaic, although it might *appear* naturalistic. Prose is for ordinary, verse for extraordinary. In one scene prose can shift to verse (and back again), and when it does you can be sure that some raising of the emotional temperature is indicated. It denotes an elevation, subtle but unmistakeable, of both the quality of thought and the intensity of feeling. It *feels* like poetry; it usually is if it feels like it.

In case verse frightens you, just remember that the iambic pentameter is a perfectly natural speech rhythm in English, just as the Alexandrine fits the rhythms of French to a T. If you were ever to gush at your beloved: "Shall I compare thee to a summer's day?" he might question the content, but the form would seem unremarkable. (Mind you, try not to be carried away in Delhi; a summer's day there is hell.)

In Act I, Scene v of *Twelfth Night*, notice how Viola, the moment she sees what a dangerously beautiful creature Olivia is, leaves behind her bantering prose and siphons her pained approbation into verse. Her jealousy is transmuted into formalised male gallantry, and the effort requires verse to express it:

> 'Tis beauty truly blent, whose red and white
> Nature's own sweet and cunning hand laid on:
> Lady, you are the cruel'st she alive,
> If you will lead these graces to the grave,
> And leave the world no copy.

Olivia, flirting rather than threatened, continues to speak in prose until the end of the scene. But at last, when she is thoroughly roused by her intriguing visitor, she too breaks into impatient verse:

> Get you to your lord;
> I cannot love him: let him send no more;
> Unless, perchance, you come to me again,
> To tell me how he takes it. Fare you well:
> I thank you for your pains: spend this for me.

Disjointed, nervy, definitely disturbed by an unfamiliar excitement, the verse structure tells us what we need to know of her state of mind.

You can't hang about with verse; the thought begins where the line begins, and it ends when the thought ends. There is no time to prepare yourself; you have to hold your nose and jump. That might entail sustaining an idea for eight or ten lines of blank verse, which is why being able to control a large chestful of air brings dividends. If you are able to express a huge thought on one breath so it's cohesive and speedy, so much the better for the actor's control of the image and the audience's comprehension of it. You'll find the grand old actors good at this, John Gielgud pre-eminently. I once heard a recording of Sarah Bernhardt doing a thirty-line speech from *Phedre* apparently on a single breath; it was unbearably exciting, even though the recording was distorted. I'm not talking about rushing; I'm talking about clarity of thought.

Verse hands you rhythms on a plate, and if you short-change it by missing a beat, you will feel it. It is, for that reason, easier to learn. It is also easier to learn because the choice of words is so very out of the ordinary, and also, obviously enough, because the shape of the verse on the page catches the eye. The lines don't run on; the lines of verse make a surging pattern on the page.

Prose is more difficult to commit to memory, probably because it is a tad closer to our everyday speech. In that sense verse is the less quotidian and the more musical of the two. However, I don't wish to stress the difference too much because all major plays have rigourous constructions you would be wise to heed.

Harold Pinter is quite as concentrated and structured as Webster. In 1966, I was in a production of Harold Pinter's *The Birthday Party* directed by the author himself. Where Webster has iambic pentameters as the skeletal structure supporting the poetry, Pinter has punctuation as a prime structural element for his prose. One day Doris Hare, playing the landlady, romped through a speech of hers about corn flakes with the debonair glint of somebody who has just learned their lines off pat. The speech goes like this:

> MEG: **Those flakes? Those lovely flakes? You're a liar, a little liar. They're refreshing. It says so. For people when they get up late.**

As You Like It

Act III, Scene v

SILVIUS: Sweet Phebe, do not scorn me do not, Phebe:
   Say that you love me not; but say not so
   In bitterness. The common executioner,
   Whose heart the accustom'd sight of death makes
      hard,
   Falls not the axe upon the humbled neck
   But first begs pardon. Will you sterner be
   Than he that dies and lives by bloody drops?

[*Enter* ROSALIND, CELIA, *and* CORIN, *at a distance.*]

PHEBE: I would not be thy executioner:
   I fly thee, for I would not injure thee.
   Thou tell'st me there is murder in mine eye:
   'Tis pretty, sure, and very probable,
   That eyes,—that are the frail'st and softest things,
   Who shut their coward gates on atomies,—
   Should be called tyrants, butchers, murderers!
   Now I do frown on thee with all my heart;
   And if mine eyes can wound, now let them kill thee:
   Now counterfeit to swoon; why, now fall down;
   Or, if thou canst not, O, for shame, for shame,
   Lie not, to say mine eyes are murderers.
   Now show the wound mine eye hath made in thee:
   Scratch thee but with a pin, and there remains
   Some scar of it; lean but upon a rush,

(Scene continues on p. 46)

Harold jumped from his seat and shouted "No, no, Doris, I didn't write that!" She stared at him, aghast. "The full stops, the full stops, Doris; where are they?" The penny dropped. "Oooh, yes, I see," she said, and did the brief lines again with a clear full stop after each one. That brief pause after each line, utterly banal though they are meant to be, gave the speech that peculiar threatening quality that Pinter's plays generate; behind each suburban hedge lurks a madman.

In Shakespeare, there are passages which initially seem a little obscure; there is no harm whatever in translating them into colloquial speech to get the gist. Take Phebe and Silvius in *As You Like It* [facing page], although this is not a particularly difficult passage to understand.

Somewhere in the green-wood, Silvius has said "if looks could kill..." Phebe gives him the brush-off: "Since when are eyes murderers? You can see a scratch on the skin, you can see the impression of grass if you lean on it; but even though I look daggers at you, where's the mark?" And Silvius' reply: "Oh, one day, and I hope it's soon, you may fall in love with someone else and then you'll know the wounds are *inside*, and all the more painful for that." And Phebe: "Stay away till I do then, and then tease me as much as you like; but don't ever insult me with your pity, because I refuse to feel sorry for you."

There is nothing more guilt-inducing than being loved when you can't return it. Guilt leads to defensiveness and that, I think, is why Phebe spends all of seventeen lines railing about how looks *can't* kill. She sounds as if she is trying her damndest to be kind ("I would not injure thee"), but her temperament betrays her best intentions. So the emotional struggle sustains this fairly lengthy speech, and gives it fire. Here,

(Scene continued from p. 44)

> The cicatrice and capable impressure
> Thy palm some moment keeps, but now mine eyes,
> Which I have darted at thee, hurt thee not;
> Nor, I am sure, there is no force in eyes
> That can do hurt.
>
> **SILVIUS:**   O dear Phebe,
> If ever,—as that ever may be near,—
> You meet in some fresh cheek the power of fancy,
> Then shall you know the wounds invisible
> That love's keen arrows make.
>
> **PHEBE:**   But till that time
> Come not thou near me; and when that time comes
> Afflict me with thy mocks, pity me not;
> As till that time I shall not pity thee.

Measure for Measure

Act II, Scene iv

ANGELO: Ha! Fie, these filthy vices! It were as good
To pardon him that hath from nature stolen
A man already made, as to remit
Their saucy sweetness that do coin heaven's image
In stamps that are forbid; 'tis all as easy
Falsely to take away a life true made
As to put metal in restrained means
To make a false one.

too, is your "Newtonian" theory at work, between "the pale complexion of true love, And the red glow of scorn and proud disdain." (If you want to have a go at paraphrasing something infinitely more demanding, try Angelo's speech from *Measure for Measure* on the facing page. Good luck.)

Perhaps you have noticed that very often in Shakespeare, the more heated the emotional temperature, the more talkative the character. Of course there are most honourable exceptions; one of the most haunting springs to mind: Cleopatra's unadorned "Pardon, pardon" when Antony storms at her for her cowardice. ("Newton" again.) This verbosity is so very opposite to our own monosyllabic attempts to express our feelings, but then plays are not life; the gift of the gab should be reveled in, not shied away from.

Just because so much language is flying around, the less you "paw the air," the more the words will have their rightful clarity. Be still; then the words will come from a still place. Be still; then your concentration will be inner instead of outer. If your hands are lunging about, put them in your pockets. If that feels like you're cheating, who cares? At this early stage the work is for you, to help you realise the pleasure of *words*, and to thrive, dolphin-like, in that new element

Deprived of the writer's gift of finding *le mot juste*, we lesser mortals fiddle and doodle and um and er, while our hands go on a desperate quest in lieu of our minds; a messy business. But art brings order to quotidian chaos; using someone else's words is a very different matter from using your own. The language becomes a physical experience if it is used to its utmost expressiveness. Sniff the aroma of the language, chew the words, roll them around, spit them out; taste the vowels and relish the consonants; enjoy them.

Talking to yourself can be extremely fruitful while working out what on earth is going on. Talk aloud in rehearsal if you like; some of the best actors do it. Ask yourself whether your character is lying or telling the truth, or, indeed, whether your interlocutor is. Ask yourself whether your character knows, or cares, whether he or she is telling an untruth. Ask yourself if you believe what you have just uttered, or whether there might not be another slant to the line, and so on. Get the Geiger beeping.

When you draw a still-life, the objects take shape if you draw the space that separates them rather than the objects themselves. Just so with a play. If you talk yourself through apparent non sequiturs you might find the missing link. Comment on other character's lines: if someone says to you, "Shall I compare thee to a summer's day?" you may say to yourself "I wonder why he's flattering me?" or maybe "Pull the other one," or "More, more, tell me more." This search for emotional logic need only be the work of a day or two, but as more and more fascinating things are uncovered your first impressions will change and develop; that's what rehearsals are for. Once the rehearsals are up and running and people are catching fire from each other, there will be a different dispensation, but in the early days explore, explore. Everything I urge you to do here will be redundant with an attentive director at the helm and a good company spirit; I am merely proposing self-help for young actors.

Very early on in my career, I had the luck to witness the possibility of such flexible thinking from Paul Scofield. He came into rehearsal one morning for a ten o'clock start on a difficult play, *Timon of Athens*. While everyone was wrapped around their coffee mugs, he quietly occupied the empty rehearsal stage and ripped into a particularly troublesome soliloquy five times in five completely different ways without pausing. Coffee cups were stranded in mid-air as people stopped chatting and, mouths agape, began to watch this protean exploration. The last word in the last soliloquy was "poison," and he tilted his head back and a weird howl came from his throat on that word; the scaffolding on the stage seemed to catch the note, and I swear it trembled. Then he picked up his jacket and quietly stalked off into the greenroom, as if all he'd done was to unblock the kitchen sink. The silence was total. The actor's concentration had been awesome. It was like seeing a master gymnast limber up, with something of the same sense of spiritual isolation. He was not aware he was being watched, or if he was, he didn't care. What he was doing was working out five different thought-plans for the speech, all valid, to see which one suited him, and the play, best. Actors are there to serve the play.

In a soliloquy, the stage is yours, and sharing your thoughts with the audience is paramount. The audience becomes your intimate, you take them with you, you confide in them. Their silence feeds your power. A solitary actor sharing a problem with his audience is indeed a powerful being; their undivided attention encourages confession, controlled confession. You *make* them listen. Inner concentration.

In long speeches within a scene, however, it is the pressure of your *need* to speak which keeps the other character(s) quiet. If you pause for too long, he or she would be free to jump in with their bit. So there is a feeling that if you don't say what you've got to say, you might burst. I am not talking of tenseness here, I am talking of the Shakespearean character's *desire* to speak, at length and at speed.

With this in mind, it is very often helpful to quicken your thinking process while working things out; it's amazing how bogged down one can get with too much pondering. (Paradoxically, the actor can never think *too* precisely on the event.) One seems to lose courage somehow—Hamlet is right. The next word seems insurmountable. So go for the jumps like a brave horse, all the while seeming to have just arrived at the thought. It has to shout "eureka!" however quiet the speech. We shall look at an example of what I mean when we work on Benedick's soliloquy.

Don't, for heaven's sake, assume a "poetical" voice just because you're speaking in blank verse. Stop "acting" and allow the words their own power of expression. You will have less to do yourself. Easier said than done, I know, but it might as well be said. Our Russian pianist learned the way from a wise colleague, and Hamlet counseled against tearing a passion to tatters; I'm in good company. I recall a production of *Hamlet* where this counsel was well and truly ignored by the actor playing Claudius, who ranted and shouted his way through the part, while the Prince observed all the subtlety and fluidity of presentation he had advised in his speech to the Players. One could not help concluding that Hamlet was the better actor, both within and without the play.

Avoid expiring your breath before a blank verse line, for two reasons. First, it leads you into hesitation, which makes plunging into the line more hazardous: it gives you time to spot the dangers. Second, it expends your energy; all the energy that should have gone into the line is now down the drain. Exhaling before you speak is a way of signaling, albeit unintentionally, the emotional colour of the line. There's no need to semaphore; the words will manage to convey the emotion, thank you very much. That's what they're there to do! So, for instance, if you (as Phebe) feel like groaning with exasperation at Silvius' craven plea for kindness, don't. Hold it in. Let your exasperation feed into the line:

I would not be thy executioner...

I don't want to appear disheartening but the fact is that the people in Shakespeare's plays are more intense and vivid than we are, and to avoid watering them down to our own relative pallor it needs to cost the actor something. The greater the play, the greater the talents required to do it justice. I love it when things seem to matter terrifically to a character. Drama, after all, is about people in crisis. When we drop in on the world of a play, it should feel much like a prawn being popped into a cauldron. People in plays are always getting into hot water.

When we work on scenes, searching for the comfortable way (and by that I don't mean easy; I mean that it sits well), we cannot help asking ourselves all kinds of twentieth-century questions: Why does she fall in love with such an idiot? Where have I just come from? Why is he so gullible? Who was my mother? (not such a daft inquiry since none of the girls in the comedies seem to have one), and so on and so forth.

It's natural enough; we are post-Freudians, after all. Life is awash with pop-psychologists and lay interpreters of human frailty. Going to a shrink has become an unexceptionable pastime. Everyone seems willing to offer half-digested rationalizations for everyone else's behaviour.

But there are times, in the comedies, when asking too many questions will get you nowhere. People fall in love boom-bang, just like that. Over the edge they hurtle, careening through the air and splashing into the ocean, where they must swim valiantly towards dry land...and marriage. We derive untold pleasure from seeing interesting people getting into trouble, then fighting their way out of it. In *As You Like It* the whole "falling" bit is taken at sublime face value as Rosalind and Orlando fall for each other at a wrestling match. They are aware:

> ROSALIND: **Sir, you have wrestled well, and over-**
> **thrown**
> **More than your enemies...**

> ORLANDO: **...O poor Orlando! thou are over-**
> **thrown:**
> **Or Charles, or something weaker, masters**
> **thee.**

Sometimes a character will have an unrealistically dominant attribute that defies any attempt at rational explanation. It is quite simply *necessary* for the play; there is a Good Duke and a Wicked Duke in *As You Like It*; there is nasty Don John in *Much Ado*. Their nastiness or goodness acts as a catalyst for the necessary action of the play. Those who have these extreme natures just have them, and that's that. Choleric, needlessly vengeful, malign: go for it. The larger the character, the more wayward and varied their natures. The gigantic enigma of Iago's vengefulness takes one's breath away with:

> **He hath a daily beauty in his life.**
> **That makes me ugly.**

Nowadays "insecurity" is the all-purpose excuse for rotten behaviour, but you wouldn't get very far by allowing Iago that soppy waiver.

Once, long ago, I was rehearsing the scene where Lady Anne is wooed by Richard III over the hearse of her newly-dead husband. It's an infuriating scene to come to terms with for a modern actress. I kept searching for a reason why she succumbs to such a transparent overture from the malevolent man who murdered her husband. An exasperated Peter Hall found an economy for me one fine day: "Don't ask why; just ******* do it!" was the gist of his note. It was a help, actually. It forced me to plump for the simple answer: sex.

The lovers in the comedies have a "daily beauty" in their lives times a thousand. As they swim in that ocean they've tumbled into, we need to see every stroke they take in order to keep their heads above water. For the great ones it has "an unknown bottom, like the Bay of Portugal. It cannot be sounded." There are no half-measures in Shakespeare's lovers.

No wonder, then, that these plays are so glorious to work on; they are exhilarating, life-giving creations. Tussle with the double meanings, revel in the antitheses, dance from the light into the dark and out again into the sun. Such creatures cannot be shied away from but must be embraced in all their lunacy. They are quick-witted, ironical, valiant individuals, with great hearts and generous temperaments. It's all there in the words.

All of their minds work with amazing dexterity: I think it would be true to say that the deeper their feelings, the quicker they think. In everyday life we make a myriad instantaneous judgements in a second; when danger threatens we make them in a nano-second. We make such decisions because our antennae are on the look-out for the slightest threat to our survival. The characters in a play are also on a life-threatening course; think of it that way, at least.

Intellect and passion are entwined in great writing. When an actor addresses such extremities he or she must achieve the same fearless symbiosis. An acting intelligence is not necessarily an intellectual one by any means, but it's an extraordinary attribute all the same. It can give the impression of great intellectual grasp while still retaining its innocence. It is both cunning and inventive. I have to say I do not know any actor of the first rank who is stupid. Ignorant, maybe; stupid, no.

Shakespeare requires you to use your intelligence. Only when your head comprehends precisely the meaning will the emotions, "like greyhounds in the slips," be able to run free and easy. Otherwise they will be strangled in mental muddle, "full of sound and fury, / signifying nothing," like that ranting Claudius.

"Honouring" the language, using it to its utmost both in meaning and in execution, allows the emotive power of words their full value. It is the vowels that act as the conduit for emotion; clip them, shorten them, give them short shrift, and the emotions will have a constipated journey. The more open and flexible they are, the more the consonants can be used as choppers and sling-shots to send them on their way.

I suppose it's true to say that I instinctively knew that anyway, but I discovered how crucially the vowels affect the speaking of blank verse when I was directing the *Othello* I have mentioned. John Kani (he who was Othello) and I did very intensive work on the text together. He was attempting to compress the work of years into a few weeks: he had never acted in Shakespeare before in his life. He had suffered a grossly inadequate education under apartheid. Most crucially, English is not his mother-tongue, although that was exactly what I wanted for Othello; the foreigner, the exotic, the "wheeling stranger of here and everywhere." In English, the Xhosa accent tends to compress some vowels and elongate others: "eth" for earth, "stet" for state, "hev" for have, "eet" for it, and so on. There's nothing wrong with this in everyday life, but in the poetic uplands of blank verse these shortened vowels were hindering John, in spite of his being the most articulate and vivid English-speaker I know.

As we worked on the part, and as his familiarity with its language and his assurance in the playing of it grew, so too did those recalcitrant vowels. The diphthongs began to make themselves known. The "r"s sneaked in to round them up, and now, instead of a constricted "haht," a released "heart" began to beat. Vowels now began to be the lightning-rods for his feelings; the force was grounded instead of random, full-blooded instead of short-circuited. I am still haunted by what came out of him with the word "anthropophagai," and the howl of "O, blood, Iago, blood!..." He was magnificent.

Othello: John Kani as Othello, Joanna Weinberg as
Desdemona (The Market Theater, Johannesberg, 1987)

Indeed, the whole cast profited from the verse work we all
did, as most of them were in the same boat, never having done
any Shakespeare either. But John's journey was that much
harder. What he achieved was a resounding triumph for this
"honouring" of the language, and gave proof positive that generous vowels allow the blood of English at its mightiest a free
and generous flow.

Elizabethan actors would have been more aware of certain poetic devices than modern actors, and would have responded instinctively to demands in the verse such as assonances, antitheses, puns, and word-play. Their ears were not as dulled as ours are to the infinite variety of rich language. But we have to be reminded to sharpen our linguistic perceptions, and bring not only common sense back into play, but the desire to astonish the listener with the excitements of highly-wrought images. Once you are aware of what is there in the verse and how to use it, you may discard what you will; that is your prerogative, but you must be *aware* of what you are discarding. A trapeze artist knows to within a millimetre what dictates the impression of ease he gives as he hurtles about at those vertiginous heights. His seeming effortlessness is the product of fine judgement, accurate practise, and repeated experience.

There is no point in prioritising a list of what the actor must attend to in speaking blank verse, but I would guess that first and foremost he must *tell the story*.

"Shakespeare's plays, like iron filings to a magnet, seem to attract any crisis that is in the air." I can't recall who said that, but it's true, and that is why his plays continue to be done all over the world. It is particularly true in repressive regimes, where the metaphors of the plays speak volumes. The story of a black man and a white girl, deeply in love, whose marriage is destroyed by Iago just because he feels like it, had profound resonances in a South Africa where Mandela had not yet walked free. If you read Iago's speech to Othello, Act III, Scene iii, lines 231–241, you will find a justification for the theory of grand apartheid as cogent and ill-conceived as any Calvinist polemicist could cook up; Shakespeare seems to be toying with entrenched ideas of bigotry centuries before it was put into practise by a Nationalist government and made constitutional. I suppose you might define apartheid as the view that miscegenation is unnatural, and indeed the first third of *Othello* is much taken up with the idea of "erring from nature." Brabantio, the father of she who is thought to have erred, is your typical armchair liberal, for whom it is OK to invite a black man to dinner, but woe betide he should marry your daughter!

The cast made this tragedy accessible to an audience, largely Sowetan, that had probably never seen a Shakespearean play before. They managed to do that because they made the language theirs; they felt at home with it. And *that* was because we worked on the text so thoroughly, and in such detail, that not one of the actors, in the end, felt intimidated by it.

That work produced the happy opposite of what I have always dreaded: a deadly, awestruck silence, where an audience feels they are being "improved" in some way by imbibing "culture." This is usually the province of well-behaved, Ivory Snow-white urban audiences. Not so in Johannesburg, where the audiences at The Market Theatre are mixed, and hence wonderfully vociferous and volatile. Tragedy, in Africa, is not a conventional form in the theatre, although God knows it is on the streets. They are inclined to laugh when you least expect it, firstly because they are not trained to the decorum expected of an audience attending a tragedy in Europe, and secondly because no tragedy on the stage could come near to the outrageous callousness of the tragedies they were experiencing in their lives every day of the week. Those laughs were disconcerting, but they forced the actors to keep a tight rein, discarding any excesses that might endanger their credibility. All to the good, say I. With a comedy you know if it's working because either you get your laughs or you don't, which keeps you on your toes like anything. However, while serious plays tread just as fine a line, participation by the audience has more muddled parameters.

Othello does not patronise its audience by simplifying an abhorrent racism, but rather traces a course of utter destruction—destruction by whim, if you like—in great poetry, giving it the size and anguish that such terrible wantonness merits. No such great poetry was around to take the measure of the wanton destruction that apartheid spawned. This play could attempt it for us. Thus Shakespeare's vision found its time and place. Othello can no longer, I believe, be played by a white actor. It would be neither fitting nor dignified nor believable. "Thus the whirligig of time brings in its revenges"—thank God.

Much Ado About Nothing: Alan Howard as Benedick and
Janet Suzman as Beatrice (Stratford, 1967)

Photo by Harlald Photographic Services

Much Ado About Nothing

Now let's look at Benedick's speech from *Much Ado*. Ewen and then Andrew, both very different personalities, had a go at this, and each brought to it a delightfully individual quality: Ewen street-wise, laconic, unexcitable; Andrew romantic, word-hungry, eager.

The scene has Benedick—hidden behind a shrub, up a tree, wherever—eavesdropping on his pals and Leonardo gossiping about Beatrice's unrequited love for him. The audience knows it's a set-up; Benedick (ready for love, but damned if he'll admit to such foolishness) doesn't.

When they divine the bait is swallowed, the perpetrators depart, with full marks for asinine acting honours. Beatrice hasn't yet had the same trick played on her, but her turn will come.

The delight of this scene is its mistaken motive: the plotters believe that Beatrice and Benedick truly are chalk and cheese:

> **The sport will be when they hold one an opinion
> of another's dotage, and no such matter;
> that's the scene that I would see...**

says Don Pedro to Leonato.

Much Ado About Nothing

Act II, Scene iii

BENEDICK: This can be no trick. The conference was sadly borne. They have the truth of this from Hero. They seem to pity the lady; it seems her affections have their full bent. Love me! why, it must be requited. I hear how I am censured: they say I will bear myself proudly if I perceive the love come from her; they say, too, that she will rather die than give any sign of affection. I did never think to marry. I must not seem proud. Happy are they that hear their detractions and can put them to mending. They say the lady is fair; 'tis a truth, I can bear them witness: and virtuous—'tis so, I cannot reprove it; and wise, but for loving me. By my troth, it is no addition to her wit; nor no great argument of her folly, for I will be horribly in love with her. I may chance have some odd quirks and remnants of wit broken on me because I have railed so long against marriage; but doth not the appetite alter? A man loves the meat in his youth that he cannot endure in his age. Shall quips, and sentences, and these paper bullets of the brain awe a man from the career of his humour? No: the world must be peopled. When I said I would die a bachelor I did not think I should live till I were married. Here comes Beatrice. By this day, she's a fair lady: I do spy some marks of love in her.

Beatrice and Benedick, on the other hand, don't know (or won't admit) that the reason they react so strongly to each other is because deep down it's love. They have become a double act from way back, and can't get out of it. The plotters unwittingly allow them to.

For our actors, Ewen and Andrew, bravery was required. Reading a passage out loud for the first time can be hell. The difference between thinking about something and actually doing it is both minute and huge. An audience, to a nervous actor, seems judgemental, sitting there watchful and silent. But it's as well to remember that an audience wants things to go well too; they want to enjoy themselves.

Like the speech, this exercise is also a set-up. What should take as long as it needs has to be quite falsely accelerated, like a speeded-up shot of a flower opening. So I crave your indulgence, Ewen and Andrew, if I appear to force you before you are ready. But I promise you, you will have nothing to lose by working faster than is comfortable, and who knows, there may be some gains. I once rehearsed for a production of *Three Sisters* in three weeks flat, which is breakneck speed for Chekhov, and it turned out rather well, to everyone's surprise. In this game, you run the race you have to run.

So what kind of a speech do we have here? [Facing page.] It's in prose, because Benedick is not yet ready for poetry. It's largely monosyllabic, because he's just suffered a shock to the system, and is trying to collect his thoughts. It's a soliloquy, so he is free to confide things to the audience which he hardly dares confide to himself. It is Benedick's third soliloquy, so we will learn more of what goes on under that amused exterior than we ever have before.

It is as tightly packed as a parcel of wood-shavings; tautly constructed, compact. It proceeds from the external Benedick to the internal Benedick with amazing speed, like a pneumatic-drill cracking the surface of the sidewalk to expose the cables beneath.

(Herein lies its deceptiveness; it is a speech that seems to be without much complication, because it has spirit and dash and some obvious comedy, and given those attributes Ewen and Andrew both made enough sense of it at first go; enough, but not enough. Like acidulous old Jacques, I cry "More, I prithee, more.")

When Benedick comes out of hiding, the actor needs to decide precisely whom he is addressing with that first line. Imagine the audience as *one* person rather than a host of disparate people out there in the dark, a person you trust enough to reveal your innermost thoughts to.

Imagine that person as waiting for you to speak, and you're happy to find a willing listener. Or if you like, imagine that person as innocently passing by, and like The Ancient Mariner, you stop them; whatever. There is an optimum moment for speech to begin, and if you miss the moment, it's quite tricky to catch another, while still stoked up with all the inner pressure that Benedick's discovery has engendered in him.

Play a game: imagine, as you emerge from your bush, that you hear a ball coming at you, whooshing through the air; now mentally lob it back from whence it came, from your friend, the audience. The smack of the strings on the ball is the optimum moment. (This is not a bad analogy, actually. I was always told that acting is like a tennis match; lobs, smashes, mean little drop shots, cross-court volleys, smooth returns straight down the line, back-hand spins, surprises at the net. In an ideal world, that sort of on-your-toes attitude should prevail with ensemble work. In a soliloquy you make the going; you're on your own.)

If you look at the play, you will see that Benedick has had seven lines to absorb what he's overheard: from Leonato's formal:

My lord, will you walk? dinner is ready

to Don Pedro's mischievous

Let us send her to call him in to dinner.

So the actor ought to be well and truly itching to start right away.

This can be no trick.

The short, sharp words brook no denial. They reinforce the shock. They seem to have equal value. (But he's shrewd enough to know his friends are capable of playing tricks, otherwise he wouldn't venture the word.) These monosyllables will do for the actor roughly what dotted crotchets will do for the pianist: it's an indication, anyway, of hard consonantal sounds rather than fluid ones.

Proof of it being no trick: "The conference" —business-like word— "was sadly borne." Longer vowels here—he's recalling the sobriety of it. "Sadly"? — "seriously"; long faces, concerned voices. (They were discreet with their winks and nudges.) So it can't be a trick because the conference was mightily serious.

They have the truth of this from Hero.

And is she trustworthy? Virtue itself. (Everyone has to think that, otherwise the plot couldn't work.) Both Hero and Beatrice have impeccable credentials in the morals department.

They seem to pity the lady.

Which lady? Hero or Beatrice? Of course, Beatrice. Who else is at the forefront of our mind? "Pity"—strong word, disturbing. Not exactly a flattering reflection on Benedick as the object of her affections. And these "affections" of hers seem to be pretty serious.

. . . it seems her affections have their full bent.

"Full bent," eh? That's a whole heap of affection. That indicates a great curving arc of the stuff, strained to its utmost. (Cupid's omniscient bow creeps in as an image).

(He thinks . . . "Do they pity her because she loves me, Benedick, or simply because she's suffering any old pang of unrequited love? My darkest suspicion is the former; the blighters are actually sorry for her loving *me*. Humph . . .")

Love me!

"Little ol' me?" A shift from the distancing pedantry of "it seems her affections have their full bent" to the plain charged Anglo-Saxon "love me." The penny has dropped with a clang. A new and astonishing scenario opens up: reciprocation, responsibility, coupledom . . . Might there be the merest pause between "love" and "me," as if he can't believe his luck?

. . . why, [*thinking time; "do I draw back from the brink, or take the jump?"*] **it must be requited.**

Very gentlemanly, that. Not "I must requite it," but the passive "it must be requited." We're still a little hesitant here; even perhaps a little grudging? The thought of all the teasing that will no doubt follow is rather daunting to a chap whose reputation is that of a confirmed bachelor, a free spirit. Still, it's a pretty magnanimous offer all in all; makes a chap feel good.

Alternatively, that

why, it must be requited

could be read as a hugely chivalric gesture, much being made of the generous assonances in the "i" sounds:

WHY . . . requWHYted.

I hear how I am censured

Self-examination now: unnerving to hear yourself discussed by your intimates. There's bit of a seesaw going on here. A touch of righteous indignation? Or might a note of martyrish concurrence creep in?

. . . they say I will bear myself proudly . . .

Proud to us has a rather glamorous Flamencan air about it; flaring nostrils, tossing hair, that sort of thing. To the Elizabethans it was snootier; arrogant, stiff-necked, and, in Benedick's case, the wrong thing to be.

. . . if I perceive the love come from her [*for "if" read "when"*].

. . . they say, too, that she will rather die than give any sign of affection.

("Mmm—sounds familiar . . . sort of thing I do.") Look to the end of the speech; once this thought has taken hold it persuades him to read Beatrice's face all wrong.

Joy from the audience; what fun to hear him unconsciously describe her as he would describe himself. His excitement is mounting here. Thoughts zoom to marriage . . .

I did never think to marry.

True or false?

1) Never thought he'd find anyone good enough for him to marry? OR

2) Marriage, the institution, goes against the grain? OR

3) Of course he's thought about it, but never admitted it? OR

4) This is just the public defense he can't relinquish even in private?

He's already told us earlier in the play that the woman he requires couldn't exist, so high are his criteria. But is it true, or just Benedick's bluster? Ewen suggests, interestingly, that he is looking for the feminine equivalent of his own self-image.

Now that the notion of marriage has come home, most enticingly, to roost, the idea grows more intriguing because it's not just anybody, it's Beatrice.

So, a little self-improvement is indicated:

I must not seem proud.

("On New Years Day I am giving up smoking forever.") He

means it, he has indeed heard how he is censured. And, as Ewen nicely observes, he means it even if he doesn't mean it. Put that in your pipe and smoke it.

To temper the unaccustomed pliability, he becomes a little self-congratulatory:

> **Happy are they who hear their detractions and can put them to mending.**

("Not everybody is superior enough to do this sort of thing, y'know.") Do we detect, ironically enough, the merest touch of arrogance as he says this?

Or is there a certain real humility in the line; a quiet determination to change his ways? (Actors must be able to turn on a sixpence, emotionally speaking. The millionaire, Nubar Gulbenkian, who owned a London taxi, was purported to have said: "My car can turn on a sixpence, whatever that may be.")

("Can't seem to get this girl out of my head"):

> **They say the lady is fair . . .**

But she's still kept at arms length, by the passive use of "they." He might have said "I *know* the lady is fair." Is this because he fears rejection? So this sentence about Beatrice's qualities retains that fearful, rather formal, tenor, almost like a man reading a sales catalogue. He can't bring himself to say "she's beautiful, she's honest, she's clever, I adore her"; it's too much for him just yet. He must keep his emotion at bay; circle round it; sniff the heady aroma of perfection.

He does manage, however, the grace to put himself down with a vulnerable:

...wise, but for loving me.

Or could he be fishing for compliments from his audience?

That unaccustomed attack of the vulnerables needs correction badly, so a fervent expletive follows:

By my troth...

("Dammit! —it's neither very clever of her nor very foolish of her, because—watch out! —I'm going to love her back"...)

...I will be horribly in love with her.

I dare any actor worth his salt not to have a high old time with "horribly." I mean, what a writer: "wildly," "insanely," "passionately"—nothing even comes close to "horribly." You get the impression that Benedick searches for the right word to describe the sheer folly of his commitment, as if there's an indrawn breath while he scans the Oxford Dictionary until "H" for "horribly" appears—and almost expires with the relief of finding it. Of course it is also perfect comic bathos.

(There's a feeling of a Maserati revving at the lights from here on).

And now, as if inspired by "horribly," look at the splat of gritty words thrown up by those racing tires:

"quirks," "remnants," "railed," "quips," "career"...

Who would picture humour having a career? But that's what he's made his name on, being Benedick the Joker; you always have a good time with Benedick. Lovely juxtaposition: "career" (vroom!)/ "humour" (grin). Also "career" denotes speed, danger, verve. And remember the Elizabethan "humour"; the thrust of your nature.

And what about the sparky:

... odd quips and remnants of wit broken on me ...

("Sticks and stones may break my bones but words will never hurt me.")

If we care to look more closely, we see how he protects himself by belittling Beatrice's projected witticisms:

odd quips

—as if she only finds them accidentally, like driftwood—

and remnants

—frayed cuttings off a larger piece of cloth.

He gets better and better at justifying the imminent birth of the New Benedick:

A man loves the meat in his youth he cannot endure in his age.

That's a matter of fact, and perhaps it should be said matter-of-factly.

The more he can project himself to himself as a chap who is doing the right thing by returning Beatrice's affection simply as a matter of form, the less he has to confront the disturbing idea that he might be just a man like any other.

Best of all:

> **... paper bullets ...**

Now there's a surreal image that would have made Salvador Dali fall to his creaking old knees with gratitude.

> **paper bullets of the brain**

—an irresistible alliteration that should crack out from the gun-barrel with explosive relish.

And what about:

> **... awe a man ... ?**

He neatly aggrandizes the male of the species, while Beatrice's little stings are diminished to irritating mosquitoes ready for the swatter. Has "awe" ever been used so pointedly as an active verb before or since, I wonder?

Now we're headed at full speed into the winning straight with:

> **NO: THE WORLD MUST BE PEOPLED.**

If it were in fifty-foot neon in Times Square, it would light up the whole of Broadway: BENEDICK'S APOLOGIA it would scream.

Do leopards change their spots? If they're in love it looks as if they do. It's all a question of priority: does Benedick care more about his public image or his personal future? Does he deny what he has been in order to prepare the way for what will be? This is the essence of the struggle in the speech.

The most endearingly transparent piece of self-justification of all clears the path:

When I said I would die a bachelor I did not think I should live till I were married.

"Die," "live": it's as important as that.

The scene could have ended there; Benedick could have run off to gales of laughter, and the play would roll on. But something much better happens.

Shock, horror! The object of his affections stomps in; cross as could be at having to leave the dinner table to look for Benedick, frowning like the devil, mad as a snake. Beatrice is confronted, unaccountably, by an asinine fellow smiling all over his face.

I do spy some marks of love in her

confides our hero to his friend, the audience, while a bemused but ever combative Beatrice plays the old game; knives out, mockery at the ready.

. . . fair lady . . .

"Fair" has a more lyrical quality than we think of nowadays; it is a stronger attribute, ascribing beauty to the inside as well as the outside of a beloved person.

By this day—

It has to be a gorgeous sun-filled Tuscan summer, and Beatrice is the embodiment of it. Mind you, even if it were pouring rain, Benedick would still have the sun shining.

Much Ado About Nothing: Alan Howard as Benedick and
Janet Suzman as Beatrice (Stratford, 1967)

I do spy some marks of love in her—

"Spy" is good; secret clues are sought by a love-stricken voyeur
secretly scanning the wrathful demeanor of his beloved; a con-
fidence shared with the audience, which is all the funnier for
being wrong. The extent of his mistake is wonderfully borne
out by the scene that ensues between the two of them.

All I have done is to make us aware of the structure and probable content of the speech. There will be other readings, all perfectly valid provided the essential nature of Benedick is honoured. That nature, obviously, will be filtered through the personality of the actor playing it.

Benedick lives by his wits and is, in some sense, the quintessential Shakespearean comedic character. He wields words as weapons with the same spirit of enjoyment a jock feels as he dons his football gear, or a boxer his gloves. Ewen, Andrew, and I were intent on targeting specific words and releasing that same relish by imagining why and how each of them were chosen.

We are using naturalistic means to achieve an unnaturalistic end. We analyse the literary devices, familiarize ourselves with their intent, give ourselves well-founded choices, explore alternatives based on textual clues, and so on. We are then able to reach out towards heightened speech, extravagant concepts, and singular phraseology without sounding hollow or contrived. All good plays require this sort of groundwork, but Shakespeare is the Big Daddy of 'em all.

I can't stress often enough, though, that the more layers of meaning, intention, motive, self-discovery, etc. that are found, the better. If you don't hunt down the singularity of its component parts, the speech as a whole cannot attain singularity. Things Are Not Quite What They Seem; the motto to remember.

Textual mastery liberates the voice, the actor's Stradivarius. It responds to clarification with the same eagerness as the mind, because the emotions have an unimpeded conduit once the debris of obfuscation and generalisation has been cleared away.

For Ewen and Andrew to begin cold on a speech of this heat was damnably difficult, so it was necessary to warm up with all kinds of shenanigans, like whirling round on each fresh thought, or chucking the lines between them at speed as in tennis, or whispering to break a "tune," or shouting to get the blood up and running, or crawling from under furniture. In fairness, all that sort of improvisational thing should be left until the speech is well under the belt. So I offer my warm admiration to them both for the courage with which they offered themselves up, to both me and the audience.

Comic acting relies largely on what an actor can do with a specific word to make it funny. The only time I ever saw Edith Evans on the stage was at a solo recital she gave when she was a very old lady, audacious in pink taffeta, and it seemed as if the entire acting profession had turned up to witness this rare event. Sitting in my row was Anna Massey, who leaned forward just as the lights dimmed, and whispered loudly to me: "I've come here for "dwindle," what have you come for?" (She was referring to one of Evans' most spectacularly comic performances in *The Way of the World* with that famous speech ending "...I shall by degrees dwindle into a wife.") I guess we had all come for "dwindle," really, though some more conventional souls might have come for "handbag." People would travel, too, to hear what Maggie Smith did with "haddock" in the breakfast scene in *Hay Fever*. Mrs. Malaprop and Dogberry, for instance, are parts constructed entirely round the misuse of words, the former out of pretension, the latter out of ignorance.

Now, I am not advocating any old-fashioned actorish games with words; far from it. But there is a quirk that some actors have that enables them to spot the intrinsic funniness in a word and to convey the character's attitude to life through that word. Of course, the writer did it first, but where would he be without the actor making much of it?

The stage can take this sort of verbal hyperbole; film cannot. If you were to see Laurence Olivier's Othello you would be struck, perhaps, as I was, by how theatrical his performance is on the screen. His speaking of the verse is impeccable, of course, and it is vivid and lacerating, but it is too much for the camera to take. That camera is always spying out the land for lips that hardly move, and eyes that speak volumes; consequently it was Frank Finlay's quieter Iago that it sided with.

I am, I must confess, not that keen on the idea that stage performances should be recorded on film, even for the archive. Even though I myself made a video film of *Othello*, I am doubtful of the use to students of the theatre. To later generations they have a fusty air about them, and you can't help wondering what all the fuss was about. They cannot capture the atmosphere in the auditorium, nor the power of the actor's presence on the stage, nor the feeling of *place* that is so vital to the communal act of witnessing, which is the essence of theatre.

Peter Brook is fascinated with the special power a specific place exerts on performance. In 1970 we went to Persia, as it was then called, to see his unforgettable production of *Orghast*. The questions that he and his group of actors were asking themselves were interesting: Is there a special sound to tragedy? Why do certain languages seem able to express the tragic mode (Greek, Russian, English) more flexibly than others? Can a specific emotion be communicated solely by sound, like music? Is it the meaning of the words, or the timbre of them as they are uttered that is conveying that emotion? Are there core themes (jealousy, revenge, fear of the gods...) that are universal to all peoples, and that can be universally understood? To help them explore these inquiries into the nature of the tragic scenario, Brook and and the poet Ted Hughes devised a language based on Ancient Greek, Senecan Latin, and an ancient Zoroastrian priestly language called Avesta. This made-up language had a past, present, and future tense, I'm told, and could therefore carry generational ideas well enough. Above all, what this invention did possess, weighted with the authenticity of its illustrious origins, was the means to make weird and wonderful noises to express emotions, although, and this was the point of the experiment, absolutely no one except the performers could understand cognitively what was being said.

A great navy sky arched over our heads, splintered with icy white stars. The invited audience climbed the ancient stone steps that wound through the ruins of Persepolis, and up and ever upwards to the tomb of Ata-Xerxes sitting high above. The stairway was lit by guttering oil lamps, which cast flickers of warm light on the bearded profiles of libation-bearers carved into the stone on either side. We all whispered, awed by the age and might of this ancient city carved by a dead civilization into the rocks of the desert. We sat quietly before the huge carved frontage of the royal tomb, bas reliefs of great beauty incised into its rockface.

Irene Worth (now there's a great actress!) played the Jocasta figure. I wish I could recall the name of the actor playing Prometheus, a tough, pugnacious, crouched figure, like a hairy Atlas burdened with the weight of the great gift he had found: fire. But I do recall the drama of it: a great ball of flames was slowly lowered on a winch from the top of the tomb-face, illuminating the heiratic carvings with a red and golden glow as it crept downwards, until it was caught in a huge bronze bowl held aloft by the primitive figure waiting for it at the bottom. It was with a mixture of tenderness and terror that he held that primal ball of fire; it seemed he had captured the sun itself. The black desert sky was totally silent as this remarkable image played itself out, as if shocked at the theft of its jewel.

It was a distillation of a poetic metaphor second to none; that of man discovering the prime source of energy in the world. It was great theatre. In the end, the language was redundant. Glimpses of crouched and keening figures dwarfed by the mountains and the sky, of mouths stretched wide with an unnamed grief, of arms stretching in supplication or anger to the fiery heavens remain in the mind's eye. And, much later on, a final, unforgettable image of a man leading a white cow with a bell around its neck, unhurriedly (in the way of cows) through the vast floor of The Valley of the Kings, just as rosy-fingered dawn touched the gigantic tombs of Darius and Xerxes with a wash of pink.

I have to remember, as I eulogize the experience, that even though we didn't know exactly what the protagonists in this remarkable experiment were saying, they did. Their bodies were informed with the tragedy that they were unfolding to us, and that is why I remember their haunting shapes so vividly, in that setting blooded with history. Edith Evans' imaginary sculpture has a reverberation after all.

The power of the theatre is that it resides in the memory, and is burned on the retina of a member of the audience. A stage performance comes alive by being witnessed then and there, and then it's over, and a different thing happens on Tuesday.

I say this with some feeling, because there is certainly no performance of mine that I can view years later with any equanimity. I look at a Cleopatra I did for the television and I shudder, not out of any false modesty, believe me, but because I have changed, and what I did with that part when I was younger I would not do now. No comparison here, but I was told a story by a friend of mine, who was a friend of Greta Garbo's, that one day he took her to a retrospective of her films at The Metropolitan Museum in New York. He told me how she sat there, all hunched up, watching herself and muttering, in the third person "Now she's good. No, no, now she's bad. Now she's terrible. Yes, now she's OK..." That was her prerogative; she saw how she had changed, too, and to hell with the fact that her films are classics of their kind. I symphathise; performances are reflections of their time and are written in water, even though the film as a whole may have a lasting impact. There must be a new Hamlet each year; last year's Hamlet is last year's Hamlet.

The best *Hamlet* by far that I have ever seen was Buzz Goodbody's production for the RSC, in 1976, with Ben Kingsley (before he became famous) and a wonderfully involved cast. It was a production that seemed to understand the play very profoundly, and it unwound its mysteries with effortless ease, like a broad river running slowly and majestically towards a dark ocean. It was funny and it was heartbreaking; I don't know what lock was picked to open the door so widely on its profundities. The fact that Buzz most tragically killed herself just before it opened may have meant that she had understood something unknowable about death, and invested her production with an uncanny knowledge of it. That thought haunts the mind. *Hamlet* is, at its very heart, a play about death. Like a black diamond, hold it up to the light and every facet reflects another meditation on the subject. I saw it twice, because I couldn't believe that it seemed to make such sense of the play the first time. The second time, months later, was just as intense an experience, so I knew it wasn't just me feeling shattered about Buzz; it was the production. My tears ran unheeded down my face for that revelatory four-hours-traffic of the stage, but I know that if I saw a film of it now, I would wonder what madness took me. It is best left alone, in my memory and in countless others'.

These are mysteries, and it is as well to be reminded that nothing of any real importance can be said in a book like this. When I talk about the drudgery it takes to begin working in an ordered and specific manner on a piece of Shakespearean text, I can in no wise intimate what that might lead to. It might even lead to the ground being properly prepared for inspiration to occur at a later stage; then our work will have been worthwhile. Inspiration does occur sometimes, but it is not easy to talk about. It is the only thing that makes sense of this incredibly frustrating profession.

Effort leads to effortlessness; you learn to think so that you can stop thinking.

There can be an entire performance which is seized by a feeling of ease and effortlessness, almost as if you, the actor, had nothing to do with it. The performance seems to play itself. Or there can be sections of a play which suddenly yield up their secrets to you where before they had seemed intractable. Sometimes an audience is aware that something out of the ordinary is happening, and it will be unforgettable to them in later hours and years. Sometimes it is only the actor who gets taken by this unlooked-for event, and the audience remains unaware of anything special happening. It doesn't matter; it is a private incident which you can hug to yourself, knowing that creative inspiration is a fact and not a fiction. It is always inspiriting and thrilling.

I once had to fetch my dear friend Peggy Ashcroft from a theatre where she was performing in an Albee play. When I came into her dressing-room, she was weeping and laughing all at once, and she said to me, "It happened, it happened!" I knew what she meant instantly. It took her hours to come down from that high.

How did I know what she meant? I have been particularly lucky in my life in the matter of great teachers, or, more properly, those people who have opened "magic casements ... on the foam of perilous seas, in faery lands forlorn." John Barton was certainly one of those whom I love and revere, though he'd humph all that nonsense away with a beard-y smile. (If you really want to know what's what, I exhort you to read John Barton's *Playing Shakespeare*. Anything I may have to offer is merely a pale reflection of that.) His lessons on the sonnets, which he would snatch between shows, after shows, and during shows up at Stratford-on-Avon in the early sixties, were revelatory. The most complicated conceits would unravel to yield up their secrets under his easy-going critical eye. Shakespeare seems as easy as pie to John, and he dumps his enthusiasm on your head like a bucket of spring water. It was John who edited the three parts of *Henry VI* so brilliantly, turning them into the two plays which kicked off the great Quartercentenary season in 1964. So seamless were his rewrites and interpolations and simplifications that it was mooted we should hold a Spot-the-Bard competition to see if even the most knowledgeable aficionado could pick out Barton from Shakespeare. He is the only academic who is a true theatre animal, who enjoys plotting deadly sword-fights quite as much as he enjoys delving for character through text analysis. He has been a huge influence on the playing of Shakespeare over the last thirty years. Combined with Peter Hall's entrepreneurial genius, their *Wars of the Roses* signal the beginning of modern attitudes to Shakespeare: ensemble play-ing, pragmatism, textual accuracy, natural speech contained within and enhanced by a strict blank verse structuralism, and a concomitant physical loosening up.

Mind you, I had had a pretty fair education before, and was in love with the English language before I ever came to England. The two teachers I had at drama school were, like all great teachers, slightly eccentric. Michael MacOwan was the principal of LAMDA (London Academy of Music and Dramatic Art), and was terrifically unsentimental and puckish in his approach to Shakespeare; he could stand no nonsense, and hated "acting" even more. Anything which smacked of the voice beautiful was mocked away by an endearing chuckle. The voice teacher there was the great Iris Warren, a rather dauntingly booming sort of figure, but she coaxed her students towards simplicity like a dog herding sheep; sniffing out the least hint of pretension, and dol-ing out doses of Zen philosophy like fresh scones.

My first experience if "it" happening was under her tute-lage one winter afternoon at school. A gloomy gray sky low-ered through the skylight, the sodium lights of the street cast their yellowed shadows; it had been a long week. She had given me a speech of Cleopatra's to work on:

> **Sir, I will eat no meat, I'll not drink, sir;**
> **If idle talk will once be necessary,**

I'll not sleep neither: this mortal house I'll ruin,
Do Caesar what he can. Know, sir, that I
Will not wait pinion'd at your master's court;
Nor once be chastis'd with the sober eye
Of dull Octavia. Shall they hoist me up,
And show me to the shouting varletry
Of censuring Rome? Rather a ditch in Egypt
Be gentle grave unto me! rather on Nilus' mud
Lay me stark nak'd, and let the water-flies
Blow me into abhorring! rather make
My country's high pyramides my gibbet,
And hang me up in chains!

(Act V, Scene ii)

The extremity of it panicked me; I did the normal thing and raved and shouted. Rubbish, it was rubbish. Meaningless blather. Iris got me to whisper this speech, which is rather hard to do, because you still feel you must communicate it, and the whisper becomes harsh and urgent. No, just the words on the breath like a sigh; thoughtful, gentle, no pushing. What the Queen was actually saying began to make sense to my fevered brain, I *heard* her internally. Very gradually she got me to add a little more voice, and a little more, until a real human being seemed to be speaking. As darkness fell on that classroom, Janet had disappeared and it was Cleopatra talking. It became an effortless transition. I remember feeling very light and relaxed as if another person had taken control and relieved me of a burden, and at the same time freed me to my charge: the speech was mine to do whatever I wanted with.

You don't forget an experience like that, because although it may sound suspiciously like a woolly spiritual revelation, it is, in

Photo by Reg Wilson

Antony and Cleopatra: Janet Suzman as
Cleopatra (Stratford & Aldwych, 1973)

fact, a very specific and powerful one. If you can do that once,
you can surely do it again. After the dust had settled, I knew that
I could be an actor after all, and that it wasn't entirely a hit-and-
miss affair. You are super-aware in a heightened state like that;
there is nothing mindless about it, even though your mind is
wholly given over into the capable hands of your instinct. You
become so much the Queen of Egypt that saying "my country's
high pyramides" doesn't embarrass either you or the listener.

Years later, when I was playing Cleopatra at Stratford, I
remember Peter Brook coming to a preview and giving me a
short, sharp reminder of that very thing. He described a
thought with his hands, and pondered, and edited internally,
and then the blue eyes twinkled, and he came out with the
briefest note ever given to an actor. "Dynasty" is all he said.
And he didn't mean Joan Collins, either.

Photo by Douglas H. Jeffery

The Relapse: Janet Suzman as Bernthia (Aldwych, 1966)

Twelfth Night

Again and again in Shakespeare's plays the theme of appearance and reality is addressed.

> JACQUES: **Invest me in my motley; give me leave**
> **To speak my mind, and I will through and**
> **through**
> **Cleanse the foul body of the infected world,**
> **If they will patiently receive my medicine.**

And again:

> **My lungs began to crow like chanticleer,**
> **That fools should be so deep-contemplative**

And Viola pondering on Feste:

> **This fellow's wise enough to play the fool;**
> **And, to do that well, craves a kind of wit:**
> **He must observe their mood on whom he jests,**
> **The quality of persons, and the time;**
> **And, like the haggard, check at every feather**
> **That comes before his eye. This is a practice**
> **As full of labour as a wise man's art:**

> **For folly, that he wisely shows, is fit;**
> **But wise men, folly-fallen, quite taint their wit.**

Lear loves his Fool, who, via riddles and jingles, offers honest insights allowed to neither courtiers nor, tragically, daughters. He is no threat to the king, holding no office. Beatrice, from behind the safe haven of a mask, jumps at making mock of Benedick to his face. Conversely, the masked Romeo and Juliet are instantly magnetised; barefaced, their true identities would have tempered that initial attraction. Hamlet, affecting madness, acquires the license to speak and to observe in a way that sanity would otherwise preclude. Rosalind, disguised as a boy, can test the character of Orlando to an extent she never could as a girl. Portia, dressed as an advocate, can enter a man's world, exercise her considerable competence, and rescue her lover in the process. Bassanio's thoughts on which casket to choose is a highly wrought dissertation on values and judgements. Henry V, disguised, goes amongst his soldiers to test their mood before the battle of Agincourt, which provokes in him an uncharacteristic bout of introspection. Katharina adopts a rebellious outside to protect a tender inside, and only Petruchio has the perception to see beyond the adolescent braggadocio. He, in turn, challenges her with an assumed, and ridiculous, persona to get what he wants; Katharina's love and loyalty.

One could go on and on . . .

That is one of the chief functions of disguise; it is to teach you as much about yourself as about others. The girls, especially, who dress as boys achieve a heady freedom which allows them to discover the deepest recesses of their own natures. Simultaneously they are able to observe the behavior of others without the encumbrance of having to behave as men expect them to. Shakespeare understood the strictures and frustrations of spirited women, and allowed them the intoxication of liberation. This may seem paradoxically anti-feminist, because it is only dressed as men that they taste freedom. I would counter that view by saying that they revert to being women all the more eagerly for having traduced their own natures for a brief, yet highly instructive, time.

So here we have Viola dressed, of necessity, as a page, delivering a message from the man that she loves, to the woman that he loves. What a ghastly ordeal.

Illyria...Never-Never Land...a land buoyed up by Love. If love didn't exist it would surely deflate and sink beneath the waves like Elos. Everybody is busy sending frantic love-semaphores to somebody else: Malvolio to Olivia, Olivia to Cesario/Sebastian, Antonio to Sebastian/Cesario, Orsino to Olivia, Viola to Orsino...*La Ronde.* This is not a land of jobs, or politics, or sheep-shearing; this is a land where people have nothing better to do than while away the charged time with song and booze and self-deceiving yearnings.

So here's Olivia, bored no doubt; a rich girl with nothing much to do all day but pursue a show of mourning for a dead brother. (The number of plays where a woman with nothing better to do is ripe for trouble...from the Phaedra's and the Phedre's, to the Hedda's and the Masha's, the list is significant; the readiness is all.) She is told that a saucy young fellow has arrived at her gates bearing the umpteenth message of undying love from the Duke Orsino. Her idling attention is caught, she agrees to see the lad. Veronica and Anne-Marie uncovered many

Twelfth Night

Act I, Scene v

[*Re-enter* MARIA.]

OLIVIA: Give me my veil: come, throw it o'er my face;
We'll once more hear Orsino's embassy.

[*Enter* VIOLA.]

VIOLA: The honourable lady of the house, which is she?

OLIVIA: Speak to me, I shall answer for her. Your will?

VIOLA: Most radiant, exquisite, and unmatchable beauty,—I pray you, tell me if this be the lady of the house,
for I never saw her. I would be loath to cast away my
speech; for, besides that it is excellently well penned, I
have taken great pains to con it. Good beauties, let me
sustain no scorn; I am very comptible, even to the least
sinister usage.

OLIVIA: Whence came you, sir?

VIOLA: I can say little more than I have studied, and that
question's out of my part. Good gentle one, give me
modest assurance, if you be the lady of the house, that
I may proceed in my speech.

OLIVIA: Are you a comedian?

VIOLA: No, my profound heart; and yet, by the very fangs
of malice, I swear I am not that I play. Are you the lady
of the house?

OLIVIA: If I do not usurp myself, I am.

(*Scene continues on p. 92*)

subtleties in this scene, so I can but give a distillation of our discoveries; mere suggestions for approaching the confrontation.

A tedious day suddenly has possibilities; Olivia decides to
play a trick, and amuse herself at someone's expense, and so we
have her first line:

> **Give me my veil: come, throw it o'er my face;**
> **We'll once more hear Orsino's embassy.**

Shakespeare's mischief again . . . the veiling gives her a way
of observing without being seen to do so; it affords her protection by underlining her state of mourning. It also whets the
audience's appetite for Viola's entrance. Maria, too, is now
privy to the fun, for fun it will be to play a trick. Why not have
Maria veiled too, to compound the difficulty?

These two lines also make it clear how little Olivia cares for
these repeated embassages from Orsino; she opts for making
the tedious formalities bearable by making them amusing.
Thus she ducks turning the messenger away unheard; bad form
at the best of times. You see how much we have learned about
Olivia in only two lines? Someone here is ripe for trouble.

What of Viola, meanwhile? How does the actor ready herself before coming on? One thing's for sure; Viola is at a terrible disadvantage. She's in love and that makes her vulnerable.
She must be feeling edgy at the thought of meeting The Other
Woman. She is also aware that she will have to pass muster as
a boy, knowing that women are inclined to notice the small
things, like walks and voices, more than men. So far she is
brazening it out splendidly, but amongst males. The imminent
meeting with Olivia is going to be tougher. The role of messenger is an unaccustomed one that she has had to assume on

(Scene continued from p. 90)

VIOLA: Most certain, if you are she, you do usurp yourself; for what is yours to bestow is not yours to reserve. But this is from my commission: I will on with my speech in your praise, and then show you the heart of my message.

OLIVIA: Come to what is important in't: I forgive you the praise.

VIOLA: Alas, I took great pains to study it, and 'tis poetical.

OLIVIA: It is the more like to be feigned; I pray you keep it in. I heard you were saucy at my gates; and allowed your approach, rather to wonder at you than to hear you. If you be not mad, be gone; if you have reason, be brief: 'tis not that time of moon with me to make one in so skipping a dialogue.

MARIA: Will you hoist sail, sir? here lies your way.

VIOLA: No good swabber; I am to hull here a little longer. Some mollification for your giant, sweet Lady.

OLIVIA: Tell me your mind.

VIOLA: I am a messenger.

OLIVIA: Sure, you have some hideous matter to deliver, when the courtesy of it is so fearful. Speak your office.

VIOLA: It alone concerns your ear. I bring no overture of war, no taxation of homage; I hold the olive in my hand: my words are as full of peace as matter.

OLIVIA: Yet you began rudely. What are you? what would you?

(Scene continues on p. 94)

the nerve-racked walk from palazzo to palazzo. And not merely messenger, but court poet: Cyrano-like she has dashed off a Petrarchan love sonnet in praise of Olivia (since her beloved Orsino is clearly poem-ed out), and learned it by heart.

Keen to get the formalities out of the way, and curious to assess the opposition, loyalty and jealousy are jostling for position as she strides in. And is instantly stymied: two veiled blobs confront her inquiring gaze. (Does she detect the faintest tremor of mirth in the air?)

Caught in the headlights, her defense is attack; she is forthright with her inquiry:

The honourable lady of the house, which is she?

The agonizing scene is under way.

After a brave flourish on the first line of her poem, Viola loses heart and asks the blob who didn't speak for information:

I pray you, tell me if this be the lady of the house, for I never saw her.

Silence ...

A little spurt of anger sparks up in Viola at her wasted efforts:

I would be loath to cast away my speech ...

et seq.

Silence again ...

Change of tack:

(Scene continued from p. 92)

VIOLA: The rudeness that hath appeared in me have I learned from my entertainment. What I am and what I would are as secret as maidenhead: to your ears divinity; to any other's, profanation.

OLIVIA: Give us the place alone: we will hear this divinity. [*Exit* MARIA.] Now, sir, what is your text?

VIOLA: Most sweet lady,—

OLIVIA: A comfortable doctrine, and much may be said of it. Where lies your text?

VIOLA: In Orsino's bosom.

OLIVIA: In his bosom? In what chapter of his bosom?

VIOLA: To answer by the method, in the first of his heart.

OLIVIA: O, I have read it; it is heresy. Have you no more to say?

VIOLA: Good madam, let me see your face.

OLIVIA: Have you any commission from your lord to negotiate with my face? you are now out of your text: but we will draw the curtain and show you the picture. Look you, sir, such a one I was this present. Is't not well done?

VIOLA: Excellently done, if God did all.

OLIVIA: 'Tis in grain, sir; 'twill endure wind and weather.

VIOLA: 'Tis beauty truly blent, whose red and white
Nature's own sweet and cunning hand laid on:
Lady, you are the cruel'st she alive,

(Scene continues on p. 96)

Good beauties [*flattery she hopes will get her every-where*] **let me sustain no scorn;** [*are they gig-gling, then?*] **I am very comptible** [*"vulnerable," "sensitive"*] **even to the least sinister usage.**

(Well, it is pretty "sinister" having two hidden faces staring your way, and "usage" is quite the right word to describe the bad joke.)

An equally forthright line from the speaking blob breaks the teasing silence:

Whence came you, sir?

Viola takes refuge in her acting role (Shakespeare often invokes the theatre as a metaphor; the obvious example being Jacques' famous speech), and chides the blob for her haughty question. For one thing, she is desperate to recite her poem before she forgets it. She's got actor's panic:

Good gentle one, [*better play safe*], **give me modest assurance,** |*modest my foot*| **if you be the lady of the house,** [*well, she's done all the speaking so far*] **that I may proceed in my speech** [*before I forget the bloody thing*].

Olivia and Maria find that funny:

Are you a comedian?

It is unsettling to be laughed at, especially on such precarious ground:

No, my profound heart.

(Scene continued from p. 94)

If you will lead these graces to the grave,
And leave the world no copy.

OLIVIA: O, sir, I will not be so hard-hearted; I will give out
divers schedules of my beauty. It shall be inventoried;
and every particle and utensil labelled to my will: as,
item, two lips indifferent red; item, two gray eyes with
lids to them; item, one neck, one chin, and so forth.
Were you sent hither to praise me?

VIOLA: I see you what you are: you are too proud;
But if you were the devil, you are fair.
My lord and master loves you. O, such love
Could be but recompens'd though you were crown'd
The nonpareil of beauty!

OLIVIA: How does he love me?

VIOLA: With adorations, with fertile tears,
With groans that thunder love, with sighs of fire.

OLIVIA: Your lord does know my mind, I cannot love him:
Yet I suppose him virtuous, know him noble,
Of great estate, of fresh and stainless youth;
In voices well divulged, free, learn'd and valiant,
And, in dimension and the shape of nature,
A gracious person: but yet I cannot love him;
He might have took his answer long ago.

VIOLA: If I did love you in my master's flame,
With such a suffering, such a deadly life,
In your denial I would find no sense,
I would not understand it.

(Scene continues on p. 98)

is wrung from her. (Truth: Viola definitely has one of those.)

Their treatment of her seems positively malicious; she chooses to be as enigmatic as they are to help her regain her self-confidence:

> **...by the very fangs of malice, I swear I am not that I play.**

Another theatre joke.

"Fangs of malice" is pretty good: they must indeed appear nightmarish to her. That's how nervous she is.

A smart reply from Olivia:

> **If I do not usurp myself, I am.**

elicits a smart rap on the knuckles from Viola:

> **Most certain, if you are she, you do usurp yourself; for what is yours to bestow is not yours to reserve.**

Since she is of equal social status, Viola's breeding can't help slipping out, like dust from under a carpet. What does Olivia detect there?

Viola quickly recovers her assumed persona, however, with a self-adjusting BUT...:

> **But this is from [*beyond*] my commission.**

She is, like an eager actor, keen to show off her own poetry, delaying the inevitable moment when she must speak Orsino's.

(Scene continued from p. 96)

OLIVIA: Why, what would you?

VIOLA: Make me a willow cabin at your gate,
    And call upon my soul within the house;
    Write loyal cantons of contemned love,
    And sing them loud, even in the dead of night;
    Holla your name to the reverberate hills,
    And make the babbling gossip of the air
    Cry out Olivia! O, you should not rest
    Between the elements of air and earth,
    But you should pity me.

OLIVIA: You might do much. What is your parentage?

VIOLA: Above my fortunes, yet my state is well:
    I am a gentleman.

OLIVIA: Get you to your lord;
    I cannot love him: let him send no more;
    Unless, perchance, you come to me again,
    To tell me how he takes it. Fare you well:
    I thank you for your pains: spend this for me.

VIOLA: I am no fee'd post, lady; keep your purse;
    My master, not myself, lacks recompense.
    Love make his heart of flint that you shall love;
    And let your fervour, like my master's, be
    Placed in contempt! Farewell, fair cruelty.

    [*Exit* VIOLA.]

But Olivia is not for being wooed with sonnetry. Her experience is that if it's poetry it's sure to be rubbish, which is no great recommendation for Orsino's previous attempts. Olivia is not taken in by Orsino's euphemisms; she smells a certain hollowness in his pursuit of her. She'd rather get the dreary stuff out of the way as quickly as she can:

> **Come to what is important in't: I forgive you the praise.**

Viola is suitably miffed; a sweet moment of poetic avidity:

> **Alas, I took great pains to study it, AND** [*let me tell you madam it's not half bad*] **'tis poetical.**

Olivia is unmoved, and brusquer than before:

> **It is the more like to be feigned; I pray you keep it in**

et seq.

One can't help feeling that Orsino's previous poems have been pole-axingly dull. (I've sometimes harbored the heretical suspicion that Hedda Gabler might have done Lovborg' posthumous reputation a great favor by burning his book; but this is from *my* commission.)

Olivia is clearly a girl used to having her own way; there's an imperious tone here that would send a lesser mortal scurrying out the door:

> **If you be not mad, be gone...**

et seq.

But Viola (manfully) stands her ground.

Maria, wary of her mistress' temper, is provoked into assisting, and, for some reason best known to herself, decides to cast Viola as the inept captain of a drifting ship.

Viola demotes her, on the turn, to a mere deck-hand; the nautical image continues with an announcement that she intends to

> **... hull here a little longer.**

"Soften up your bouncer" might be the rough gist of her next line. It is tempting to think of Maria as being a diminutive little creature, Viola teasing her with "giant." If she's not, "give the big girl a tip and get rid of her" would be an acceptable joke.

Viola is regaining her composure and beginning to run the show.

Olivia is sufficiently amused by the exchange to adjust her tone to a more friendly request for enlightenment:

> **Tell me your mind.**

Not, you will note, "your *master's* mind" She has seen that the "boy" is not easily crushed; she likes what she sees.

Viola, knowing that the message she is on her honour to deliver is intimate, and seeing that Maria is an impediment to that intimacy, goes for enigma:

> **I am a messenger.**

No more than that. Messengers usually bring bad news. It sounds serious, slightly disturbing. Olivia is increasingly curious.

This interchange of two short lines between the two of them feels like a turning point. Olivia wants to know more; Viola's not telling.

Viola wins the little tussle, by giving as good as she gets:

The rudeness that hath appeared in me have I learned from my entertainment.

Touché. Double edge to "entertainment": "I have been used by you as mere entertainment", and "you have (socially) entertained me rudely."

Olivia has the wisdom to ignore the admonition, and the curiosity to find out more. Maria is dismissed, but not without a mockingly laconic jibe at Orsino's proxy poeticisms:

...we will hear this divinity.

With the slight nervousness that occurs when two people are suddenly left alone, Olivia conducts the next exchange with wit as her sole protector, determined to live dangerously.

Viola is on the defensive, but finally can bear no more of her veiled antagonist when Olivia chooses to call Orsino's text "heresy."

She is desperate to face the truth, however threatening, and demands to see Olivia's face. Not knowing is worse than knowing.

With the self-assurance of someone who knows how good they look, Olivia, still bantering, complies:

Look you, sir, such a one I was this present. Is't not well done?

(It's tempting to suspect Olivia of wanting to show off to this boy.)

Viola, taken aback by her beauty, replies as any self-respecting woman would do under the circumstances:

Excellently done, if God did all.

Olivia, self-absorbed, fails to detect the barbed femininity of that reply, though the audience doesn't. Her self-confidence remains unassailable. It's not quite conceit, she merely affects disinterest in her own attributes as she ticks them off one by one, like a laundry list; it's the self-assurance of real beauty. She's careless of it.

Up to now, the scene has been one of immense comic possibilities: a girl dressed as a boy dutifully trying to honour her idol's commands, in the (veiled) face of hauteur and non-cooperation. You might say that frustration has been the dominant emotion.

But the scene now takes a swoop upwards to a level of anguish that only poetry can properly express. It is as if the lifting of the veil has lifted, too, the guard from Viola's poor heart. Pain transmuted to anger surges from her. She sees Olivia's face, and she sees Olivia's heart:

> **I see you what you are; you are too proud;**
> **But if you were the devil, you are fair.**
> **My lord and master loves you. O, such love**
> **Could be but recompens'd though you were**
> **   crown'd**
> **The nonpareil of beauty.**

The unfinished line (this scene is full of them) hangs hauntingly in the air.

Each stage in the scene now (Viola in the searing fire of poetry, Olivia in an increasingly sober prose) glows ever hotter in intensity of feeling, because the truth of the matter is more exposed. Viola's passionate defense of Orsino entirely overrides her assumed circumspection; she is the spokesman for her own enthralled heart, rather than his.

Olivia, to her credit, catches the new seriousness; for the first time she condescends, as it were, to poetry, and meets Viola's intensity with an equal burst of frankness. It is with some relief that we encounter a truthful Olivia:

> **Your lord does know my mind, I cannot love him . . .**

et seq.

It is such a human speech, and so pragmatic—generous in her praise of Orsino, aware of her own failure, adamantly honest—that our sympathy for her grows with each word. We have all been "adored once, too" to recall poor Sir Andrew Aguecheek's sad reflection. Her guilt-engendered generosity has a familiar ring.

But Viola is on a roll; reason has no place in her pantheon:

> **If I did love you in my master's flame** [*she is talking of herself*]
> **With such a suffering, such a deadly life,** [*unrequited love receives its just antithesis*]
> **In your denial I would find no sense,**
> **I would not understand it** [*The three strong beats hover in the accusatory air*].

Olivia, caught up in the eddies of real passion, longs to know the answer and so she asks a real question:

> **Why, what would you?** [*and thus completes the unfinished line.*]

Viola reaches into her very soul to reply, and comes out with one of the greatest love poems imaginable:

> **Make me a willow cabin at your gate . . .**

et seq. [see p. 98].

It is a great passage because the imagery is so unexpected; self-banishment to a small hut at the gates, where the days and nights are spent in an ecstasy of churning out love poems and crying out the name of the beloved, echoing to the very skies above. It is a mantra of adoration. It possesses an extremity of feeling and a single-mindedness of commitment that stops the breath.

So intensely is she experiencing her own hopeless devotion that for a split second one could feel her teetering on the edge of speaking Orsino's name when she says:

> **Holla your name to the reverberate hills,**
> **And make the babbling gossip of the air**
> **Cry out O—livia!**

(On the other hand, the actress might instead choose to speak as if she were Orsino, and so fully that it would indeed be Olivia's name that would burst from her).

That dangerous "O" is in a second transmuted to another O, of pain:

> ... Cry out Olivia! O, you should not rest
> Between the elements of air and earth,
> But you should pity me.

Again, an iamb hanging in the air at the caesura, like a buzzard...

But it looks as if the dumbstruck Olivia (as who wouldn't be?) is only capable of two unfinished lines herself. The delicacy of "You might do much" is such that it could either break the spell or prolong it. It could break it if it were a self-protectively dry comment, it could prolong it if it were a genuinely moved one.

What is certain is that Olivia is well and truly hooked (think of Phebe's reaction to Rosalind's passion.) "Who *is* this person? No mere messenger could speak like that":

> **What is your parentage?**

But Viola has shut the door on her profound heart, to protect both her pain and her privacy. She recovers, but only just, her *sang froid*:

> **Above my fortunes, yet my state is well:**
> **I am a gentleman.**

Wonderful—all a lie; all a truth.

It is Olivia's turn to lose her cool, speaking "in starts, distractedly," and so far forgetting herself as to give Viola a tip. Heavens, you don't tip a gentleman! Well, actually it's not really a tip, it's a love-token, but Viola's not meant to know that.

Viola, affronted by the gesture, and equally furious on Orsino's behalf, gives her hell and leaves. The plot thickens...

I know I have said elsewhere that too much psychological delving into the "givens" of a Shakespeare play can, at times, produce diminishing returns. If it is required that Lady Anne falls for Richard III, then that is what she has to do. As I said, I was in the end forced to opt for the simple, and most universally indefinable reason, for her doing so: sexual attraction. Fine, but she is actually a woman, falling for a man. In this scene, however, as in the *As You Like It* scenes, another scenario prevails. Here is a girl, dressed as a boy, being flirted with by a girl. In Shakespeare's day, the whole shebang was further compounded by the fact that the female parts were played by boys, so Viola would have been a boy pretending to be a girl dressed as a boy being flirted with by a boy pretending to be a girl. Whew!

After I saw Ninagawa's production of *Medea* some years ago, I understood how easy it would have been to accept this convention. The actor playing Medea had been trained from his youth in the Noh tradition of male actors assuming female parts, and it was, as might be expected, a seamless assumption. He was exquisitely female, both feline and melting, driven and seductive. Not camp, not emphasizing the usual rather vulgar excesses of feminine behavior that cabaret impersonators affect.

If any of The Globe actors were anything like as good as he was, then Cleopatra and company would have been in good hands. It must have been a man, I'm convinced, and not a boy, playing Cleopatra, or Tamora, or Hermione, or the Nurse, but for the younger parts—the boys. What a frisson it must have made when a stripling strode into that courtroom in *The Merchant of Venice* and set the place by its ears. Oh, well, that is all lost to us now, and we cannot recapture that dimension of suspending our disbelief twice over.

Sexual conflict, though, is at the very heart of these comedies, and if, four hundred years on, a contemporary director is entranced with the idea of having Olivia actually making a pass at Viola in this scene, he can be forgiven for evening up the odds by having two girls, instead of two boys, stealing a kiss, gratuitous though it may be.

While we are on the subject, Shakespeare makes it very plain when he expects an actual embrace to take place, and they are very few. They are specified textually. Here is Antony bidding farewell to Cleopatra before the battle:

> **Fare thee well, dame, whate'er becomes of me:**
> **This is a soldier's kiss:**
>
> *(Act IV, Scene iv, 1.90)*

And here is Othello greeting his Desdemona when he arrives in Cyprus:

> **I cannot speak enough of this content;**
> **It stops me here; it is too much of joy:**
> **And this, and this, the greatest discords be**
> **That e'er our hearts shall make!**
>
> *(Act II, Scene i, 1.190)*

Now that women play the women's parts, all sorts of other moments for an embrace to have a natural impetus will occur, a luxury that was carefully meted out by Shakespeare, given the convention of the times. I am awash with gratitude that he left no stage directions other than those which are embedded in the text. What glorious elasticity it gives the plays. It does, however, emphasize the fact that since we do not hear what is said with the same intensity of comprehension that his own

Bankside audiences did, a modern director will be tempted to go the whole hog. Peter Sellars, for example, elected to under-line unmistakably the love between Bassanio and Antonio in *The Merchant of Venice*, who could hardly keep their hands off each other. It gave Portia something to chew on, that's for sure.

The point I am making is that since we are bombarded with sexual allusions from morning till night, our shock level has lowered, and anything which spells out sexual excitement as graphically as possible is *de rigeur*. There is not, however, one moment of gratuitous sex in the plays of Shakespeare. Richard III decides to woo Anne, not because he cares a damn about her body, but because she will be useful to him politi-cally. Angelo in *Measure for Measure*, although he lusts after

Othello: John Kani as Othello and Joanna Weinberg as Desdemona
(The Market Theater, Johannesberg, 1987)

Isabella, puts himself through endless hoops of self-justification. Desdemona, although she elopes with Othello in a very un-nun-like manner, says:

> **I saw Othello's visage in his mind;**
> **And to his honours and his valiant parts**
> **Did I my soul and fortunes consecrate.**
> **So that, dear lords, if I be left behind,**
> **A moth of peace, and he go to the war,**
> **The rites for which I love him are bereft me,**
> **And I a heavy interim shall support**
> **By his dear absence. Let me go with him.**

No mistaking what the "rites" are, but it is a complete passion she is trying to express, and Iago's cheap smears on her character serve to enhance her dignity in our eyes. If Olivia, in the scene above, suddenly finds herself attracted to Cesario, it is not simply because there is some androgynous beauty in the boy which touches her, but because she has had a glimpse of a superior being.

Photo by Herald Photographic Services

As You Like It: Patrick Stewart as Touchstone, Janet Suzman as Rosalind, Rowena Cooper as Celia (Stratford, 1968)

As You Like It

Beware of portraying "love" with a generalised romantic wash; it is a specific emotion. The central rule of *listening* to what the other character is saying is always the best way of reacting truthfully. In life, we adjust and shift our moods according to what is said and done around us. In performance the same attention to social survival applies.

In *As You Like It*, which is choc-a-bloc full of disparate couples, think of the differences in the way the characters express their love for each other. Here's a rough-ish guide: Silvius for Phebe (dogged), Phebe for Ganymede (snobbish), Audrey for Touchstone (admiring), Phebe for Silvius (resigned), Touchstone for Audrey (raunchy), Celia for Oliver (sudden). And at the glowing centre is a smitten Rosalind telling herself that no one ever died for love, all the while dying for love herself.

Let us see what we might glean from the page. [Following page.]

Having given Phebe hell for not returning Silvius' faithful adoration, Rosalind (dressed as a boy) exits in a bit of a flurry when she notices that Phebe has taken a shine to her.

As You Like It

Act III, Scene v

ROSALIND: I pray you, do not fall in love with me,
For I am falser than vows made in wine:
Besides, I like you not. If you will know my house,
'Tis at the tuft of olives here had by.
Will you go, sister? Shepherd, ply her hard.
Come, sister. Shepherdess, look on him better,
And be not proud; though all the world could see,
None could be so abus'd in sight as he.
Come to our flock.

[*Exeunt* ROSALIND, CELIA, *and* CORIN.]

PHEBE: Dead shepherd! now I find thy saw of might;
Who ever loved that loved not at first sight?

SILVIUS: Sweet Phebe,—

PHEBE: Ha! what say'st thou, Silvius?

SILVIUS: Sweet Phebe, pity me.

PHEBE: Why, I am sorry for thee, gentle Silvius.

SILVIUS: Wherever sorrow is, relief would be:
If you do sorrow at my grief in love,
By giving love, your sorrow and my grief
Were both extermin'd.

PHEBE: Thou hast my love: is not that neighbourly?

SILVIUS: I would have you.

(Scene continues on p. 114)

Come to our flock

says she to an amused Celia as she leaves, somewhat overdoing the role of shepherd and shepherdess in her panic. It is a half-line. Phebe's next line is a complete one, so it would be legitimate for there to be a silence after Rosalind and Celia leave, as there are three missing beats in Rosalind's line. That is brilliant, dramatically; it means Rosalind's departure leaves an empty hole.

Phebe breaks this small silence with a dreamy realisation that she is smitten:

> **Dead shepherd! now I find thy saw of might:**
> ***Whoever loved that loved not at first sight.***

A saw is a saying or tale. But "Dead?" Who is dead? The "dead shepherd" is actually a reference to Christopher Marlowe, murdered in a pub in Deptford in 1593, purportedly over the payment of a bill. Shakespeare pays tribute to Marlowe again in the play, when he has Touchstone chiding Audrey with:

> **When a man's verses cannot be understood, nor**
> **a man's good wit seconded with the forward**
> **child understanding, it strikes a man more**
> **dead than a great reckoning in a little room.**

The reckoning was the bill, the check, the "great reckoning" is death itself. (There's a double meaning in that!) Marlowe wrote a popular poem called *Hero and Leander* from which the second line here ("Whoever loved," et seq.) is a quote. A very literate quote, you will agree, for a country girl. There are a couple of things to ponder on, then, with such an obscure reference:

(Scene continued from p. 112)

PHEBE: Why, that were covetousness.
    Silvius, the time was that I hated thee;
    And yet it is not that I bear thee love:
    But since that thou canst talk of love so well,
    Thy company, which erst was irksome to me,
    I will endure; and I'll employ thee too:
    But do not look for recompense
    Than thine own gladness that thou art employ'd.

SILVIUS: So holy and so perfect is my love,
    And I in such a poverty of grace,
    That I shall think it a most plenteous crop
    To glean the broken ears after the man
    That the main harvest reaps: loose now and then
    That scattered smile, and that I'll live upon.

PHEBE: Know'st thou the youth that spoke to me erewhile?

SILVIUS: Not very well; but I have met him oft;
    And he hath bought the cottage and the bounds
    That the old carlot once was master of.

PHEBE: Think not I love him, though I ask for him;
    'Tis but a peevish boy: yet he talks well;
    But what care I for words? yet words do well
    When he that speaks them pleases those that hear.
    It is a pretty youth: not very pretty:
    But, sure, he's proud; and yet his pride becomes him:
    He'll make a proper man: the best thing in him
    Is his complexion; and faster than his tongue
    Did make offence, his eye did heal it up.

(Scene continues on p. 116)

One, that since *Hero and Leander* was all the rage when it came out, even the hayseeds of Arden might have heard of the juicy bits, rather in the way *The Satanic Verses* has become a book everyone has heard of though hardly anyone has read. Two, that you might elect to ignore the literary reference (since no twentieth-century audience will have a clue anyway) and refer to poor Silvius himself as if he were yesterday's man ("dead"), usurped by Ganymede. Imagine that he might have once mournfully observed to his implacable Phebe, "Whoever loved that loved not at first sight?" Admiring the poetry, but despising the sentiment, she had impatiently brushed it off; now she suddenly finds it an apt description of her own unlooked for awakening.

If you understand what you are doing, the audience will too. The obscure references in Shakespeare don't matter too much if the modern actor has found his own scenario. Similarly, with equivocal passages, if the actor knows the story in his own mind, such is the power of theatre that he will convey his vision of it to the audience, and it will seem as if the sun has broken through.

You need to know that Phebe's speech is a couplet, and that usually rounds off or sums up a scene. That being said, the simplicity of Silvius' exposed "Sweet Phebe" (nothing more nor less) will be the first time we have heard his voice since he said [see p. 46]:

> **If ever, as that ever may be near,**
> **You meet in some fresh cheek the power of**
>   **fancy...**

And, lo and behold, she has. How agonizingly prophetic he must feel. His little line is all that, but is also a desperate plea: "hello-remember-me-even-though-I'm-invisible" sort of line.

(Scene continued from p. 114)

He is not tall; yet for his years he's tall;
His leg is but so-so; and yet 'tis well:
There was a pretty redness in his lip;
A little riper and more lusty red
Than that mix'd in his cheek; 'twas just the difference
Betwixt the constant red and mingled damask.
There be some women, Silvius, had they mark'd him
In parcels as I did, would have gone near
To fall in love with him: but, for my part,
I love him not, nor hate him not; and yet
I have more cause to hate him than to love him:
For what had he to do to chide at me?
He said mine eyes were black, and my hair black;
And, now I am remember'd, scorn'd at me:
I marvel why I answer'd not again.
But that's all one; omittance is not quittance.
I'll write to him a very taunting letter,
And thou shalt bear it; wilt thou, Silvius?

SILVIUS: Phebe, with all my heart.

PHEBE: I'll write it straight,
The matter's in my head and in my heart:
I will be bitter with him, and passing short:
Go with me, Silvius.

Phebe's reply to him is instantaneous and distracted:

Ha! What say'st thou Silvius?

It is instant because it completes Silvius' half-line: when lines are printed that way, the two half-lines become, in effect, one full line. This means there is no time to hang about thinking of a suitable reply; it is there wham-bam, an unmistakeable directive that the character is thinking quickly. It is distracted because that "Ha!" sounds very much like someone jolted out of a reverie, and coming back into the real world. It might also be a softer *Huh?*, as if to say "sorry-I-didn't-catch-what-you-said-I'm-rather-preoccupied."

Whatever it is, it is distant enough to provoke Silvius into pleading for attention:

Sweet Phebe, pity me.

(Just the thing Phebe is angered by.) His again is an incomplete line, as if his distress had rendered him wordless. The "wounds invisible" are doing their horrible worst.

To look at the line from a more objective angle, you might be struck by how infuriatingly blinkered someone helplessly in love can be; they simply can't understand how it is that their passion is not returned. You can sympathise with either or both parties at this point, depending on your own heart; Shakespeare is always very fair about his characters and their frailties and never takes sides.

This plangent little half-line is allowed to hang, as if the absent Ganymede is still invading the air with his presence.

Now Phebe concentrates her distracted thoughts. She must begin to plot her next move, keeping Silvius at a manageable distance:

Why, I am sorry for thee, gentle Silvius.

See how she deliberately dilutes the extremity of "pity" to a more manageable "sorry for." If she were to stress the "am," ever so mildly, the dilution would be seamless.

"Why" gives her a second to think, delays her reply by a hair's breadth.

"Gentle" both calms Silvius and serves to underline the contrast, in her eyes, between his self-pity and Ganymede's exhilarating put-downs. Metaphorically she is patting Silvius on the head like a puppy, in an absent-minded sort of way.

Silvius picks up on the word she has changed, "sorry," and now it is his turn to transmute plain "sorry" into a more tragic "sorrow:"

Wherever sorrow is, relief would be:
If you do sorrow at my grief in love,
By giving love, your sorrow and my grief
Were both extermin'd.

Who says the mind doesn't work with both cunning and clarity in the throes of love? His speech has an unassailable logic to it, however obsessively self-interested it may be. Yet again it concludes on a half-line, and the tiny silence that follows surely indicates a Phebe thinking furiously about how to get out of *that* one.

She manages something at once conciliatory and infuriating:

Thou hast my love: is not that neighbourly?

By putting "neighbourly" at the end, she renders the longed-for word "love" about as exciting as warm tapioca. Silvius' poor heart would surely jump and sink all in one sickening lurch. So he comes back with a wounded cry, forgetting word-play:

I would have you—

just in case the penny's not dropped yet.

Quick as a flash, (completing his half-line) she tweaks his bald declaration into a quick-witted little bridle:

Why, that were covetousness.

"Neighbors can't have what isn't theirs"; she naughtily flips the bromide respectability of "neighborly," or brotherly, love into a slap on the wrist for being greedy. "Ooh, you selfish little pig" might be the inelegant modern equivalent. Having floored him, she can now get down to brass tacks. She wants to use him and makes no bones about it; here's the job she has to offer him:

> **Silvius, the time was that I hated thee;**
> **And yet it is not that I bear thee love:**
> **But since that thou canst talk of love so well,**
> **Thy company, which erst was irksome to me,**
> **I will endure; and I'll employ thee too:**
> **But do not look for further recompense**
> **Than thine own gladness that thou art employ'd.**

The disarming frankness of the speech removes any danger of it sounding too harsh; we now know that Phebe herself has been struck by "love's keen arrows." Hence her equivalent self-interest.

If, somewhere along the line, Phebe has shot Silvius one of her ravishing smiles, it will surely help to soften the blow. Her motive is clearly to charm him into her service; reprehensible maybe, but refreshingly wicked.

Be aware how the speech has two main ideas in it: from "Silvius" to "endure" (what graciously assumed stoicism!), she will endure his company so as to hear him *talk* of things amorous. Remember Rosalind's "The sight of lovers feedeth those in love"? The *sound* of lovers will do the same for Phebe, it seems.

Then, at the caesura, she suddenly sees how she can make use of his company: "and I'll employ thee too." She's quick to add that he mustn't expect payment of any kind, either of money or reciprocated feeling. "Recompense" therefore has a double weight to it. Phebe is nothing if not an optimistic and inventive young woman.

Silvius' characteristically compliant reply, full of un-manned self-abasement, is sad but not, I think, entirely self-pitying. He'll take what he's given:

> **So holy and so perfect is my love,**
> **And I in such a poverty of grace,**
> **That I shall think it a most plenteous crop**
> **To glean the broken ears after the man**
> **That the main harvest reaps: Loose now and then**
> **A scattered smile, and that I'll live upon.**

It is only apt that a countryman should use a country metaphor to describe his subsidiary role in life, and he gives the role a certain dignity by doing so. How sad that he asks only for one of her smiles as sole recompense for this thankless job.

Lovely word, "scattered": you scatter coins to beggars. Phebe scatters smiles, seemingly as carelessly. You scatter seeds, too; the country image is continued. You also scatter killer arrows— "love's keen arrows" —and by using the verb "loose" (as from a bow), the Eros image is entrenched.

Now her smile has done its work, and she can get down to the nitty-gritty: he's caught. Her mind can revert with full concentration to the mysterious boy who has caught her fancy. Still, she retains a certain studied casualness about her question, which suggests an edge of nervousness:

> **Know'st thou the youth that spoke to me erewhile?**

Silvius tells her that he has bumped into him quite often in the forest, and more to the point, that he's rich enough to have bought a house; information not entirely without interest to Phebe. Her suspicion that Ganymede is a cut well above the usual bumpkin feeds her excitement.

Her ensuing speech is a perfect example of blank verse clearly signaling that someone is thinking in stops and starts; thinking, in effect, *as she speaks.* Almost every thought is broken midway through the verse line, at the caesura, by a contradictory one. It's an excited speech, clipping along at a terrific rate, with continually altering rhythms. Its jagged, disjointed structure is enforced by the constant use of monosyllables rather than long lyrical words. You get the feeling that

Phebe's heart is thudding with excitement as she speaks:

Think not I love him, though I ask for him...

and so forth [see p. 114].

Isn't this the mother and the father of *esprit d'escalier*, the thing you wished you'd said as you're going down the stairs?

There are no particular difficulties in this speech. The description of "black" as an insult is simply an Elizabethan fashion. Probably because the Queen was fair, they preferred blondes. It also denoted foreignness, the eternal English hang-up; xenophobes to a man. Rosalind can enjoy the put-down by pronouncing the word "black" with as many cutting consonants as she can muster, recalling as she does that "chestnut was ever the only colour."

...omittance is no quittance

is straightforward enough: "I forgot to tell him off, but he's not going to get away with it."

Lovely choices of words in the speech: "peevish," "lusty," "mingled damask," "constant red," "parcels," "chide," "taunting." Enjoy them.

Whether Phebe says the speech directly to Silvius or more to herself is an open question. I would guess the latter. It would be hard, even for Phebe, to look her stricken lover in the eye while she dissects her jolted feelings.

It's worth remembering how tricky a thing eye contact can be. You either have to be seriously in love (so Silvius' eyes would be glued to her) or lying in your teeth to hold a look for long. In between are myriad subtleties. But towards the end of the speech, when she is revving up to pay Ganymede back, Phebe might quite happily beam in on Silvius, for the simple reason that she needs him very badly to be her postman. (Ah, so here's the job she was offering him earlier.) It looks suspiciously as if she might have been sneakily plotting such a thing from way back. One of those smiles on "wilt thou, Silvius?" would clinch it. The temptation to be heartlessly seductive would beckon. I urged Emma (playing Phebe) to reach out and touch Simon (playing Silvius) on the cheek, gently but irresistibly, on this line. She jibbed at it, finding it a cruel thing to do. It is, but it is also selfish, and therefore true to the thrust of the speech. The more outrageously she behaves the better; no half-measures for our Pheeb.

Nor, it seems, for Silvius, as the poor fellow, helplessly seduced, responds with:

Phebe, with all my heart.

She doesn't hang about, but instantly begins writing a zinger of a letter in her head:

> **I'll write it straight,**
> **The matter's in my head and in my heart:**
> **I will be bitter with him, and passing short:**
> **Go with me, Silvius.**

"The matter's in my head and in my heart." That is precisely where the matter of acting Shakespearean comedy has to be; one without the other and you're sunk.

Photo courtesy Columbia Pictures

A Day in the Death of Joe Egg: Alan Bates and
Janet Suzman (Columbia Pictures, 1971)

Confucius say: No greater pleasure than seeing best friend fall off roof of house. Yes, I'm afraid so; comedy thrives on cruelty. We find it funny, no doubt because it gives us license to acknowledge our own nasty little sadistic streaks, and our own desires to take small revenges on those close to us. Excess of any kind is satisfyingly pricked by the barbs of laughter: self-delusion, pomposity, sentimentality, religiosity, overweening ardor, and ignorance are all candidates for correction. Poor ol' Silvius; spineless, doormat-ish, positively canine in his unquestioning adoration of his unattainable mistress, he deserves everything he gets from Phebe. Anyone who can't take no for an answer deserves the same. Who wants to marry a marshmallow?

And yet, and yet... There is a moral lesson for Phebe to absorb, which she certainly does by the end of the play. I believe her when she says to Silvius:

I will not eat my word, now thou art mine [*note the proviso of the New Woman; she does not say "now I am yours"*]
Thy faith my fancy to thee doth combine.

Having been perilously close to making an ass of herself, she embraces the idea of faithfulness, in the serious matter of who you marry, as a quality not to be sniffed at. So in the end, Silvius wins; he has taught her something valuable. No marshmallow he. It is now even possible to conceive of a rosy future for these two. Shakespeare's refreshing optimism, where marriage is concerned, is unassailable.

Henry VI, Part I: Janet Suzman as "La Pucelle"
(*The Wars of the Roses*, 1964/5)

Q & A

Questioner:

How do you find a balance between having too much concern with the text and enjoying too much what you are saying? Can you really enjoy yourself before you know what you are saying? How do you find that balance between the importance of the text and the other side?

JS:

The balance comes later. We are in infant, not to say embryonic, stages here. The text is our hieroglyphic; it is the only marker we have to tell us what the story is. I think if you start sliding over words instead of pinpointing the meaning, you get into the habit of, "Oh, that'll take care of itself." You can easily get sloppy, which means you generalise. The reason I have been so fastidious, probably unreasonably so, is because if you let one thing go it's all too easy for it to be accepted by the imagination as a *fait accompli*. It gets lazily taken on board, and the details are fudged. It's more exhilarating for the actors to be fluid and open to suggestions, and indeed to be vigilant about stopping themselves if they don't understand all the implications. I would rather they stopped themselves than I did.

Remember, we are not performing at this early stage, we are staking out the territory. To rehearse a Shakespearean play is to take pains to discover what precisely is going on. That's what rehearsals are for. You are right, enjoyment is the reward for knowing what you are up to. It's rather like my pianist who was having a whale of a time—too soon. What it needed was for the music to come, not through his face, but through the piano keys; to flow from the page via his eyes, his arms, his fingers, and then the piano. (Perhaps Prof. Crick will one day be able to explain that astonishing event.) A lovely circular flow of energy. Instead it was traveling upwards to his head and dissipating itself. Beethoven didn't get a look in. The pianist was describing the music rather than playing it. Just so with an actor, who can be drawn toward acting an emotion before he knows what the genesis of that emotion may be.

We are servants to these works. They need a certain humility from us. I do not mean subservience, I mean according them the respect they need to rule over our hearts and sensibilities. All the clues we have are those black marks on paper. So I think not generalising is already doing some service to the play.

Questioner:

What you have been doing all through this programme is trying to make the actors trust the text and to speak it as naturally as possible. Speaking verse is not a very natural thing to do. I'm wondering whether you feel that there are particular problems with keeping the verse as well as going for the natural, and also whether any of the actors felt inhibitions about possibly losing the verse in the course of this process.

JS:

Let's ask them.

Anne-Marie:

I feel at this very early stage it is quite difficult. You are searching, searching for sense and also trying not to lose the verse. But the sense is in the verse. So, although it's hard to keep sight of, you'll get more sense if you follow the verse.

You go through a stage where you lose the verse, and you go through a stage where you lose the sense and it all falls apart, but if you look for the truth in the sense *through* the verse it does eventually come back together again, and you understand it more from having used the verse.

JS:

I suppose what we're going through is a kind of fragmentation before putting it together. You see, when we look at the verse on the page, it's got that lovely shape; in and out it goes, like breath. And that's quite seductive. It invites you to be lyrical. I've not mentioned end-stops and lifting line endings today—no time—but lyricism without cogency is an empty exercise. The kind of groundwork we've been doing today is to make ourselves aware of the truths inherent in the thoughts—thoughts made of words. Not any old word: *that* particular word. The beauty deriving from those truths (sorry for being suspiciously Keatsian) serves no purpose without the meaning, the intention, the juxtaposition, the interplay. Therefore no singing, no patterns, no setting in concrete. Does that make sense to you?

Audience:

Yes, a lot of sense, yes. [*I heard no "no"s, so I guess there was consensus.*]

Questioner:

Someone, I think Silvius, asked "why do I love Phebe?" and you said it doesn't matter why, and you quoted an experience you had had where the director said "forget why, just do it." But surely to the character, *why* you love someone is of paramount importance?

[*The story being referred to is the Lady Anne and Richard III rehearsal where I was told to stop searching for a reason for her seduction and to accept the unreason for it.*]

JS:

As You Like It is a play supremely about Marriage. Hymen, at the end, eulogizes it, and joins the couples who are to enjoy this more or less blessed state. Without wanting to delve into the device of appearance and reality just here—a theme fascinating to Shakespeare—the central couple are empowered to discover their own natures, while the others learn to make do with what they've got. All of them are drawn to each other, who knows why; an essential chemistry is at work. That's the point at which asking too many questions gets you nowhere fast in the matter of motive. Arden, like Illyria, is a magical place where pragmatism fights for survival. Hearts just collapse, it seems, throughout this play, as frequently and as thuddingly as a wrestler falling to the mat. So instead of lingering on the "why," I suggest concentrating on the "how."

Questioner:

Silvius again; his character seems to be the weakest in the play, especially as he is so managed by a woman, but in fact he is a very strong character because he doesn't allow his love to be destroyed. How would you work on the character of Silvius to bring that out more?

JS:

This play is, as so many of Shakespeare's plays are, about the power of disguise. What truths you can utter when you are not quite yourself. "He uses his folly like a stalking horse, and under the presentation of that he shoots his wit" is an observation about Touchstone's freedom as a clown to speak home truths. Silvius is the exact opposite; he has no cover-ups, no defenses, he is undisguisedly prey to his own desires. That is probably the most difficult state to dare yourself to be in as an actor. Utterly vulnerable. Simon was beginning to understand how far there is to go in the matter of vulnerability, and I salute him for that.

Simon:

The danger of playing a character like this is not to believe it thoroughly; in other words to caricature it.

JS:

Yes, the *quality* of something rather than the thing itself. This is a difficult trap to describe to non-actors, but it is a very real danger to actors. Shall we say its like playing the game of adverbs; "lovingly," or "slowly," or "fastidiously," etc. All very well for a quick impression, but the actor must know more, much more.

What kind of "lovingly" exactly? —in an imagined scenario, does he hold his gun lovingly because it's an antique, or because he's going to kill someone he hates with it, or because he shot his first lion with it, or because it will protect him from a coming danger? Sometimes improvisation is used to encourage actors to think a scenario through accurately in their own way.

We have all the words we need in a Shakespearean play, so now we use them to help us find the exact kind of love, say, that Silvius feels for Phebe. He could appear a pathetic soul, rather than a man struggling to control his feelings. If such love is depicted as being merely the soppy end of things, then the play is not posing the argument about the tensile strength of love with the rigour that I think it intends. Love is put through various tests, like the labours of Hercules, and is expected to survive. Silvius' love turns out to be an all-forgiving, constant, and deep thing in the end; he has substance.

So now, Simon has the immensely subtle task of showing us a *smitten* man of substance, which is not possible to achieve in this class alone, but at least we have begun to investigate the richness of his character.

It is an exploration particularly hard to do in front of an audience; it needs the privacy and trust of a rehearsal room, where we do not pass judgement on a given character but allow its nature to emerge in action. The pressure of being watched at work before they are ready to be seen is hard for actors to bear with equanimity, although you, the audience, are just as important a part of the ritual of theatre when it is being performed as the actors are. Today your contribution is a strong one because you have chosen to be here out of interest in the subject. Even so, you exert an unconscious pressure on the actors.

Questioner:

You discouraged an expiration of breath before a line. Now, is that mainly for blank verse or do you find that to be a general actor no-no?

JS:

I'll stick to blank verse. I kind of like noises but it's best to make them *within* a word. However, making noises just before a line, apart from being a diversionary tactic of some kind, does something physical to you. It's usually a quite unconscious sign that the actor is groping for the feeling of the speech, and is scared of the speech itself.

Thought—the thought of the word—comes through on your breath. The stomach is the seat of feelings. That's where we feel sick, anxious, butterflies—it's where laughter begins. It is where the breath operates from. (Well, approximately from your diaphragm to below your navel.) You can see, then, that if you *exhale* before saying something you will have to *inhale* again to speak. So the thought is on the floor; you have to pick it up all over again. Needlessly effortful.

If the feeling could be expressed by just a noise, then that is what Shakespeare would have written. He does that very often anyway, from Phebe's little "Ha" to Cleopatra's great:

O! wither'd is the garland of the war,

and untold hundreds of other mighty O's.

Racine has a great line in "Ah's" but that's another story . . .

So, without wanting to labour the point too much, trust the verse. Dive in. Observe its context, and give it its full due. The plays do work after all; we have several hundred years of performance to reassure us on that score. The greater the play, the greater the expertise needed to show it off.

Questioner:

You remarked that Emma, as Phebe, began to loosen up as soon as she had a clear idea of what she was doing. Do you find that the body responds to the thoughts, or can you start with an idea of the physicality of a character?

JS:

Oh, yes, you can start with a physical idea. Sometimes a gesture, an attitude starts up an idea in your mind. Say you hold a hand out very simply, palm up, you can feel yourself assuming any amount of imagined scenarios; begging... catching a drop of water... holding an insect... asking a question... —lots of things. Then the idea engendered by the gesture can be developed if it's to lead to something useful in a character's personality. It helps the actor to be aware of how responsive an instrument his body is.

When you hit the bull's-eye, there's nothing you can't do. You could stand on your head as the character, and it would be right. Even if you're wrong, you're right, if you see what I mean. Best of all you can be still without strain; the words will have their genesis in a still, central place. Stillness doesn't mean confined, it means you are so relaxed that the body will behave economically—"suit the action to the word, the word to the action."

You will have noted that as the actors got increasingly familiar with what they were doing, hardly a gesture wasn't believably the characters'. By gesture I mean the whole of the body, not just hands and arms. Body language then becomes as much a communicator as formal language.

When the body is not at home with the thoughts, you have surely noticed the oddly disjointed gestures—palms up, hands offering to show you a place which is perfectly invisible, somewhere behind the actor's thigh? "Get thee to a nunnery," says our lad, and the helpful hand indicates a building vaguely to the left of Elsinore. It is mocked by actors themselves as being

"Shakespearean" acting, and it is always silly, but it is a common fault with young performers who think the words need spicing up.

In reply to your second query: an actor often has a physical idea of the character's nature from the word go. A private movie plays in the inner eye; you can "see" the creature. Or he/she gets an idea from somewhere outside the play; actors have been known to go to the zoo to observe animals, they watch people on buses, in pubs...whatever. There's no rule, only the search for what truly serves the character.

I began by saying that it is possible for an idea to spring from a movement, and now I am saying that movement can spring from an idea; I hope you find that creatively paradoxical but not contradictory since "both/and" rather than "either/or" can equally be contained in any discussion of the acting process.

Question:

Do you feel you can use Stanislavski's or Brecht's theories in relation to acting in Shakespeare?

JS:

Why ever not? Both practicioners have more in common than you might suspect. Both have seeped into our consciousness. A good theory is common-sense observation anyway, which is why it was a mistake to accord The Method a capital "M." It is "a" method. Stanislavski codified what good actors have always and will always do when working on a character. He was continually adapting and changing his ideas, let it be said, knowing that a theory written in concrete is a contradiction when it comes to something as personal and elusive as performing. Brecht's theories are perhaps a little more polemical, but awash with common-sense nevertheless. He was a man of the theatre; he understood. Both acknowledged contradiction, and Shakespeare is all about contradiction. Contradiction and antithesis. Contradiction, antithesis, and ambiguity.

Peter Brook, too, is *par excellence* a man of the theatre, and his work over the years gives the theatre an integrity and continuity that it would have lost without his absent presence. He reminds us what theatre is for and about, and he reminds us of its profundities and enigmas with economy and modesty.

For the rest, there are rather few directors who are interested in or capable of helping an actor to find the way. There are a lot of *metteurs en scene* directors, whose chief collaborators are their designers, and whose actors are the means to achieve the "concept." All very well for a lot of plays that are not written in blank verse, but it tends to leave young actors floundering in Shakespeare. That is one of the reasons why The Royal Shakespeare Company has again instituted verse classes for its younger members; an instructive reflection on education available in recent decades.

As to textual study, academic input can be illuminating but you can't act a thesis, though you can fruitfully ingest it. A scholarly interpretation may jog you into exploring an idea further. It might even make you so disagree that you determine to do the opposite, and that in itself can be creative. Consistency is all. If you have embarked on a creative thesis for your character that is, please God, singular, you have to justify your view textually all the way down the line, if only to yourself. The audience will be enthralled if light is shone on a familiar character. That's the trouble with Shakespeare; if it's being played in England, a whole lot of people will think they know the play. All the more reason to jog them out of that conviction.

Anne-Marie:

But some scholarly decisions you simply can't show anyone.

JS:

True. But the taste might be richer, like herbs in a casserole. Editions of Shakespeare are riddled with footnotes from generations of venerable old Editors who clarify and comment and interpret, and generally make life easier for the ignorant. The Arden Edition is the granddaddy of footnoted versions, and useful to browse through when you're stuck. But the result is that the proportion of actual text per page is irritatingly sparse, so they're no good at all for rehearsing with. Easily the best edition I have come across was printed in Capetown for Maskew Miller Longman called the Stratford Series, where all the notes are on the facing page rather than underneath the text, or buried in an appendix. I'm sure there are other editions by enlightened, if less venerable, editors, that I have *not* come across. For rehearsing, the light paperbacks that you can fold backwards and hold easily in one hand are best.

One other thing. Shakespeare is gloriously free of stage directions—bar the notorious "Exit pursued by a bear" and a few others—so it's easier to pretend each play is "an undiscovered country," as if no mortal had been there before.

Be wary of stage directions; cover them over, cross them out, blank them off, elbow them. They shackle a play to its period like nothing else does. The playwright is not necessarily the best judge of how his own play should play. There are stage directions in Chekhov, in Ibsen, in Shaw, in Tennessee Williams, ad infinitum, that you can well set aside to enable you to find your own best route. Sometimes the stage directions crept into the published text from original stagings (especially of Chekhov), so even more are they leftovers from another time, another place, another mood.

For example—to get back to Shakespeare—when the venerable Editor chooses to insert the direction "She faints" for Cleopatra, just after the death of Antony, you would be justified in querying it. Cleopatra's not exactly the fainting type. It smacks of a tired old view of what females do under duress. Does her silence necessarily indicate insensibility? So what might her silence mean instead?

Say she *withdraws* spiritually. Say the realisation that Antony has gone shocks her into silence. Say she is pervaded by a feeling of abandonment so grievous that her maids, sensing her soul's mysterious absence, are terribly frightened by it. When she "comes to" there is no feeling that she has been physically unconscious; on the contrary, she speaks with a new and devastating commitment to her dead lover. There is much to say about this weird and wonderful moment in the play, and no time to go into it here, but I hope you get my drift—question everything. Do not be satisfied with what *appears* to be obvious. Look for the more interesting alternative.

Questioner:

In addressing the idea of not being sing-song-y with the verse, and keeping concerned with naturalism, how do you then take these wonderful words and colour them and give them full value?

JS:

Aaaah. I dunno. Enjoyment? What is it that makes someone pick out a word and make it shine before you, like a fresh, new-minted thing, while others tip-toe round it as if it might bite? Relish? Or courage? Because words are powerful. Powerful objects lying around on the page like unexploded bombs, like uneaten sweetmeats. The secret of new-minting a word or an image must surely be the fresh apprehension of its meaning *in the context*. The language of a play has the power to create its own reality. "*Think*, when we talk of horses," (or cabbages or kings) "that you see them printing their proud hooves i' the receiving earth..."

John Gielgud's great talent is to make the most complex verse seem a piece of cake, at speed. All seems natural and flowing and comprehensible. He grasps the essential thoughts and magics them into your brain with what appears to be dazzling ease. I once had the pleasure of being given a very useable note by him while I was rehearsing the Trial Scene in a TV version of Shaw's *Saint Joan*. He was playing the Inquisitor. We broke for lunch, after an intractable morning where I was getting nowhere with those long Shavian sentences. He sidled up and in his imitatably subtle tones murmured: "Would you mind if I said something?" "Oh please," said I, avid for help. "I think you'll find there is only one stress per line," said the great man, and quietly wandered off to his lunch. And so there is. I pored over the text during the break, and saw that I had been greedily trying to give every word equal weight, with the result that nothing made any sense at all. It was a terse and useful tip.

You will have noticed that great performers have remarkable voices. They are remarkable because they are unstrained and expressive, and they come from the right place; not from the throat, but from what I call "the pips" —your belly, your centre. John Major has the most strangled, uncentred voice you are ever likely to hear, poor fellow. It's one of the reasons he has credibility trouble. Kristin Linklater, a one-time protégée of the remarkable voice teacher Iris Warren, probably knows more about "the pips" than anyone else in the field. Cicely Berry at the RSC also knows her onions. (They have both written books on the subject: Linklater's is called *Freeing Shakespeare's Voice*, and Berry's is called *The Actor and the Text*.) There are a few others who know how to work from the inside out, but not many. The voice is the most complex and fascinating animal. Most people's voices are screwed up, especially girls', because they are expected to repress more of themselves in life. Mrs. Thatcher screeched until she was taught how unprepossessing she sounded, but let's draw a veil...Women in public life often have a problem that men don't; the pitch of the voice seems to undermine authority. It can be dealt with, however.

I seem to be meandering...oh yes, naturalism and non-naturalism. I happen to think, as you might have gathered, that literacy is no bad thing in regard to Shakespeare, or indeed to the whole field of drama in general. It's a useful tool to be capable of recognising assonance, alliteration, metaphor, simile, antithesis. I wasn't insisting today; I didn't bring them all up. No time. But I think not to be aware of what constitutes an image, say, or a conceit, is...er...conceited. Why should one be exempt from basic literary awareness just because one is an "artist"? When you are aware of these devices it increases your response to detail, makes you more specific. Callas' acting skills were immeasurably helped by her masterful musicianship; she was nothing if not knowledgeable.

Veronica:

There is a magic time in performing when the words are no longer on the page but seeded inside you. You surprise yourself by finding a moment almost as if you yourself created that choice in that moment of time. If one reaches that stage, it is magic.

JS:

It is, yes. We're still very unfree with books in our hands—how could it be otherwise? Some people react very sensually to words straight away. They are word-mongers of some kind. They have that quirk. Others need to digest the whole thing first, and then the books go down, and then begins a whole different stage. The real business begins.

Question:

Do you find that North Americans have more trouble with Shakespeare or not?

JS:

No. I haven't found that. Although the acceptance of irony as a normal means of expression is less readily to hand in the American psyche than the English. And then there are New Yorkers...

In so many ways Shakespeare is universally ill-taught, but that he should be taught as an awesome academic study is the worst of it. The plays were written to be performed. Even if they are acted out in a messy but lively fashion in the classroom, that's a step up from the numbing drone of a teacher reading badly.

You see, in "exam mode" a cogent and well proven answer is required to a question. Certain well-tried inferences are drawn from a text, and a student, if he quotes enough, can give the impression he has thought up an acceptable answer. But in fact what is happening is that in order to prove a point, the complexities of a character are being, if not simplified, then subjugated to fit the thesis. Whereas, personified in a flesh and blood being, characters can regain their waywardness and become recognisably inexplicable again, just as the most perplexingly human people are. I don't mean muddled, I mean they satisfyingly defy simplistic definition. I heard such a nice story about Peter Hall giving Sir Ralph Richardson a note after the dress rehearsal of Ibsen's *John Gabriel Borkman*: "I've got John, Ralphy," he is purported to have said, "but where, oh where, is Gabriel?"

Now, I have nothing against scholarly disputation per se, except where it tends to bore students to death. Worse, they may find it harder, after, to come to terms with the idea of a character in a play being partly this and partly that. A black and white answer is of no use when the reply should be rainbow-coloured. I am not talking here of the upper reaches of scholarly analysis, where complexity and ambivalence are a *sine qua non*, but of youngsters whose fresh reactions are subjugated to required examination answers. The triumph of the sit-com is that human nature is crassly simplified to fit a soothing and cozy framework, and that makes people feel safe. The characters are recognisable only as stereotypes, and always tediously likable. ("Roseanne" is a bracingly dishonourable exception.) Great art is not like that at all; it opts for originality, and its alchemy makes us know we are reflections of that anarchic and three-dimensional celebration of human difference. Characters are now hateable, now lovable, changing from moment to moment. Heathcliffe is not someone you'd bump into every day, nor is Cleopatra. It is disturbing for an audience, and so it should be. Tabloid newspapers always want to sum people up tidily, crassly; no, people are more opaque and interesting than that.

Question:

What about speech? ... Is the American accent...

JS:

Much closer to Elizabethan English than our own received pronunciation, or RP as the BBC dubs it. "Gotten," rolling "r"s, and so on. I don't see any problems at all. In some ways American English has the advantage of being less tight-assed than English, and therefore less obsessed with class, and therefore more acceptably demotic. That's all to the good. If it takes away people's terror of having "posh" stuff rammed down their throats, then fine.

The only advantage British English has is its rich variety of regional dialects, all very different. (Harry Hotspur in a Northumbrian accent is always a winner.) Since the sixties, actors of the caliber of Albert Finney have unashamedly used the accent they were born with, or else a sort of mid-Atlantic kill-two-birds sound. A relief from the hot-potato bray of yore.

Questioner:

Do you ever see something you've never seen before, and say to yourself, as a working actress, "Hah, I might use that myself one day"?

JS:

Oh, actors are a pretty observant breed. You file away interesting modes of behavior seen on buses, in shops, whatever. I shocked myself one day when I realised I was watching a grieving mother on a TV news programme quite dispassionately; I caught myself thinking "so that's what grief looks like." I guess I was rehearsing something grief-stricken at the time, and it had taken over all my thinking. That's what happens— you rehearse in your head. Acting is not a profession, it's an obsession. Human behavior is utterly engrossing.

But to copy an idea slavishly is another thing altogether. You might extract the essence in order to suit it to your personality. More often than not, it will be so particular to that actor that you wouldn't be able to. Geraldine McEwan's revelatory Gertrude at Riverside Studios (with Alan Rickman as Hamlet) was so unlike any other performance of that role that I felt I had understood what made Gertrude tick for the very first time. But I would never be able to do what she did because, for one thing, my shape and my personality are so different. When Olivier borrowed a rhetorical idea from Henry Ainley it became his, and anyway he would probably have forgotten its source. I've seen some very good things happen today, but I've not put them in a drawer marked "next time"; anyway, I don't see myself playing Rosalind or Celia again... far too old!

Veronica:

When I see something really excellent I remember, not how it was done, but something of the sense with which it was done, because it has moved something in me. It's like a sense of recognition. And I know, watching you talk about or sometimes do something when talking about Celia, I go "that's good." I don't know how you're doing it or what it is, but I think "I want some of that." If I were to go away and do Celia in some production, I would hear your voice in the back of my mind somewhere saying "twinkle." It wouldn't leave me because it's perfect for the character; laconic, droll.

Questioner (an American, as it happens):

Getting back to the verse, I think the big difference between English and American actors is that there seems an innate ability in English actors to hear the exact scansion of the lines. American actors approach verse more naturalistically, and the structure, the very strict structure, goes out the window.

JS:

A pity, that. A realisation that the footage in blank verse is a help rather than a hindrance is one worth having. Scansion is not to be wrestled with like an enemy, but embraced, like a friend. Mis-scansions put my teeth on edge; you know, rather like music not coming back to the dominant. It's an indulgence to ignore structure. Would you ignore the time signature in music? What it indicates if you do is that you are not *listening* to what's been written. Were you to subject yourself to someone who massacred verse, it might be fair to conclude that he considers his individuality more important than what Shakespeare is saying. A touch self-regarding, perhaps? Anyway, it's so hard to be unresponsive to rhythm, I don't know how people can pretend it's not there.

Questioner (the same):

Well, I find that English people seem to have an understanding; it's taught in the schools. Not in America; the actual breaking down into weak and strong stresses, say, is foreign to actors there, so we get a much more vital and much more naturalistic feel; not exactly street language, but they don't adhere to the rules of verse-speaking.

JS:

Only when you know the rules well can you afford to break them. Charlie Chaplin had to be a good skater to skate badly. I'm all for an immediate, everyday, vital feel to verse-speaking. God knows, when I did *Othello* in South Africa, I had a Desdemona and an Othello who had never done Shakespeare before in their lives, so out of a five-week rehearsal period I chose to spend the entire first week on verse before we ventured up on our feet to explore the play, and it paid marvelous dividends in the end. They embraced the verse as if it really belonged in their mouths.

There's the rub; an audience shifting on its collective rear will tell you soon enough if you are being obscure or distant or false or declamatory. So I'm afraid no one can convince me that a sloppy, easy-come-easy-go attitude to verse is a benefit. On the other hand, the rhythms of blank verse are often thrillingly enhanced by a whole new generation of actors from countries who are not hide-bound by RP. I'm thinking of the lilt of Caribbean English, Irish, Hispanic, Indian, African, et al. The marvelous elasticity of English has been its greatest strength in sweeping the boards as the world-wide *lingua franca*. When Shakespeare was writing the language was growing, and he helped it grow. He loved new words, and non-English English has that same inventive thrust. That spirit can only enhance the speaking of his verse.

But please let me be clear about this; understanding the nature of blank verse and dramatic prose is no more than a means to an end, and that is to make the *content* sing out.

You see, if you think about it, structure allows you muscle, and extravagance, and bravery, and colour. It gives you a springboard from which to launch yourself into the heady heights of poetry. A sonnet is that much more powerful a verse form for being restricted to just fourteen lines; it means you have to say the maximum in the minimum of space.

Poetry is compression. Any physicist will tell you that compression yields great power. The impression of power in reserve is the single most riveting quality in a performer.

And let us remind ourselves that plays have nothing to do with real life; reality, yes, documentary realism, no. Plays are metaphors. Metaphor is poetry. Poetry is compression...

On a lighter note, here's a little jingle I remember from way back:

> **Iambic comes with steady pace**
> **Swift the trochee takes its place**
> **Next comes the dactyl on pattering feet**
> **The amphibrach next with its stressed middle**
> **beat**
> **And the last in the line, but not least, is the**
> **rare anapaest.**

Macbeth: Janet Suzman as Lady Macbeth (BBC, 1970)

AFTERWORD

These are the sort of fundamental questions that I think should be asked by an actor about his character when working on a play:

1) Who am I?

2) What am I trying to do?

3) By what means?

4) Against what resistance?

5) In order to what?

Because Shakespeare writes with such terrific depth and fluidity, the goal-posts will shift slightly during the course of a scene.

When Viola walks into Olivia's presence, her answers to these questions might be as follows: I am Cesario. I must persuade Olivia that my master truly loves her. I must present his case with fervour, although everything in me objects to doing so. I must do that to please my master. I love him so much that pleasing him is my only aim.

As the scene progresses these questions will have slightly different answers: I am Viola. I am defending Orsino's deepest feelings. I am putting myself in his shoes because I have those feelings too, and I shall express those feelings with all the power I can muster. Olivia is making light of them; she is not worthy. I must not, because I am angry, give myself away.

Only when the larger scenario is distilled down to its essential components will attention to "the moment" be allowed its due place. When the actor is clear about what he is doing and why he is doing it, the character can then express those imperatives with the words that have been assigned to him.

The still and concentrated centre from which all art flows resides in a moment, the here and now. Before you start working, do yourself a favor: give yourself time to gather your forces and concentrate your mind on the matter in hand. You have seen how tennis players pause before a serve to focus their aim; you have seen the faces of athletes at the starting block; you have seen a musician gather himself in before striking the first note. Sit quietly on a chair, doing nothing. Just sit, first as yourself, and then, imperceptibly, allow the character to enter your being. There will be a subtle change in energy. You might find yourself shifting your body to the way the character would sit. Still do nothing. Just sit there.

You will know when to stop. You will recognise when there is no more to be got out of this silent encounter as you notice your attention beginning to lose grip. It might be many minutes, it might be just a few. But at least you will have begun to make the acquaintance of a new being. The introduction will have been made. You two will have fused for a time, with no words to intervene.

These meditations on the nature of the character you wish to serve will remind you, if they do nothing else, that acting, when all's said and done, is an art. It is not to be debased by get-there-quick methods, and least of all by the judgements of the world, which is sometimes prone to pooh-pooh that which is not definable. I am not, repeat not, talking of specialness, or pomposity, or anything which smacks of self-importance, but of the vigilance and seriousness of purpose which a performer should remind himself is at the still centre of the discipline he has chosen to follow.

There is serious play, and there is playful seriousness. The quality of the thing you are doing is far more to the point than anything else.

If this sounds mawkish, I can't help it, but a recollection of the power the imagination has when it is directed to specifics is not, I hope, out of place.

JANET SUZMAN

ACTING IN SHAKESPEAREAN COMEDY

The 60 Minute BBC Master Class

"Suzman is a major classical actress... she is also a born teacher ... beneath her flame-colored hair, Suzman burned and her students duly caught fire ... she persistently came out with striking stimulating remarks (with) workshop snippets of *Much Ado, As You Like It* and *Twelfth Night."*
—Benedict Nightingale, LONDON TIMES

"Totally and incisively in charge, her unscripted preamble is a dramatic lesson in itself, with all the right places to create dramatic effect you can cut with a knife. Her dissertation on the difference between tragedy and comedy is masterly."
—Sunday Times (London)

Janet Suzman is well-known for her may theatrical, film and television appearances. She is a member of the Royal Shakespeare Company and the National Theatre Company. Equally at home in dramatic and comic roles, she is an inspiring and entertaining teacher of the thespian arts.

VIDEO: $39.95 • ISBN: 1-55783-115-7